HUDDEI IN 50 BUILDINGS

CHRISTOPHER MARSDEN & ANDREW CAVENEY

AMBERLEY

To Noah, Ruben and Orla who asked 'Why is Grandad always in the library?'
and in memory of the giants on whose shoulders we stand: Hilary Haigh
(1945–2018) and George Redmonds (1936–2018)

First published 2019

Amberley Publishing, The Hill, Stroud
Gloucestershire GL5 4EP

www.amberley-books.com

British Library Cataloguing in Publication Data.
A catalogue record for this book is available from the British Library.

ISBN 978 1 4456 7981 5 (print)
ISBN 978 1 4456 7982 2 (ebook)

Origination by Amberley Publishing.
Printed in Great Britain.

Contents

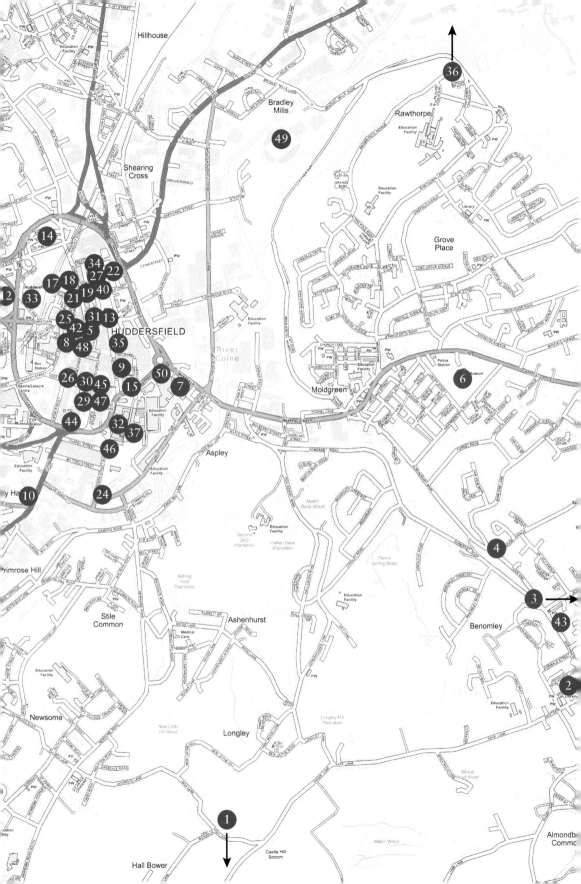

Key

Introduction

In 1068 Odersfelt, as Huddersfield was known, was reported by the Domesday Book to be 720 acres of 'waste'. Almondbury, on the hill above Huddersfield, for several centuries remained the larger and more significant of the neighbouring parishes. It had developed as a market town by the late thirteenth century.

However, Huddersfield was to grow from being farms by river crossings to a family-owned town. In 1531 William Ramsden, son of a prosperous Greetland clothier, married Joanna, the daughter of Robert Wood of Longley. Within a few years William owned Huddersfield land and buildings, his wife's land dowry and her sisters' inheritances – so began the Ramsden estate in Huddersfield.

The Manor of Huddersfield was purchased from the Crown by the Ramsden family in 1599, who then bought Almondbury Manor in 1627. The 1st Ramsden baronet was granted the Huddersfield market charter in 1671.

Huddersfield Station with fountains.

The Ramsden-owned Cloth Hall of 1766, the Sir John Ramsden Canal of the 1770s and the coming of the railway in the 1840s all led to Huddersfield's rapid expansion during the Industrial Revolution.

Control of the town by the Ramsden family was entrepreneurial and neglectful, philanthropic and exploitative, noble and mean. In the nineteenth century local government developed, dominated by the Ramsden estate, until the incorporation of the borough in 1868. The Ramsden family was still the absent landlord and freeholder of almost the whole town.

In 1920 the 4,300-acre Ramsden estate was bought by the Corporation for £1.3 million. Huddersfield had become 'The town that bought itself' and the landlord of many. In the local government reorganisation of 1974 Huddersfield ceased to be an administrative area, and was subsumed into the new multi-town Kirklees Council.

Through its industries – mining, textiles, engineering and chemicals – the town enjoyed rapid growth in the nineteenth century. In 1847 Philips wrote,

> Sixty years ago, Huddersfield now the centre of the fancy manufacture of England – was a miserable village. The houses were poor and scattered, the streets narrow, crooked and dirty … Huddersfield has grown into an important town.

In the twentieth century it was said to be the largest town in Britain, have the most Rolls-Royces per capita and the most listed buildings other than the cities of Westminster and Bath.

The local sandstone gives buildings of all types, styles and periods their distinctive colours. Its qualities have led it to be used for drystone construction, fine carving, smooth ashlar facings, roofing and paving. It is a refreshing contrast when successful designs use other materials, which are obvious when you are about the town – seven are included here. The local stone was blackened by atmospheric pollution. Since the 1950s the sandblasting and cleaning of buildings and smoke control has revealed the stone's colours.

The town benefits from the work of a few prolific nineteenth-century architects and builders who will become familiar to readers. Selective cross-references are given (the practice that developed as Abbey Hanson/Rowe/Adeas/AHR is referenced as AHR). The dates of buildings in the text are of completion or opening.

The 50 Buildings

1. Castle Hill, Castle Hill Side

In 1873 members of the British Archaeological Society visited Castle Hill and 'everyone was charmed by the extent and grandeur of the surrounding scenery and the fine view of Huddersfield'.

It is generally accepted that this very prominent steep-sided 900-foot hill has been a place of settlement for thousands of years. Neolithic remains have been found, but more evident are the earthworks that formed the defensive ring of an Iron Age fort along the crest of the hill. These were modified several times, and there is evidence of burnt palisades. These defences were remodelled for a medieval castle perhaps as early as the late eleventh century, which, as a hunting lodge, was abandoned in the fourteenth century.

In 1848 a project was announced to build a 70-foot tower observatory on the hill. By the following March it was named Victoria Tower and shares were sold to raise 1,500 guineas. Architect William Wallen displayed a model of the proposal in the George Inn. The project failed when the landowning Ramsden estate would not support it.

It was another fifty years before a tower was realised, which was to be in commemoration of Queen Victoria's Diamond Jubilee. With the support of the Ramsden estate and Corporation, the tower's cornerstone was laid on 25 June

Castle Hill, showing Norman motte with Victoria Tower and inner and outer baileys.

Above: Castle Hill and Huddersfield from above Bradford Road, 1837, by G. D. Tomlinson.

Left: Victoria Tower from the north-west.

1898. The 106-foot Victoria Tower was officially opened on 24 June 1899. It was designed by London architect Isaac Jones with construction supervised by architects Abbey and Hanson and building by Ben Graham & Sons using Crosland Hill stone with a £2,500 contract.

During the post-Second World War austerity years the tower was in disrepair and demolition was mooted. However, the tower was repaired and the finial turret removed in 1959, taking the overall hill height to less than 1,000 feet. For Queen Elizabeth's 1977 Silver Jubilee, Huddersfield Civic Society raised funds to erect a mast with a beacon, restoring the 'mountain' height.

At the time of writing there is a third planning application by the Thandi Partnership, demolisher of the Castle Hill public house, which stood in the bailey. It's seeking consent for a hilltop café/restaurant with bedrooms designed by One17.

Scheduled Monument with listed grade II tower
See also AHR 7, 30, 38, 44, 46 & 50; Graham 20–21, 25, 32 & 34; One 17, 13; Wallen 15 & 18

2. All Hallows, Westgate, Almondbury

High above Huddersfield and near Castle Hill, Almondbury was a significant village long before Huddersfield developed. It had a market charter in 1294.

The village church, All Hallows, has a complicated history. It's reputed to have Norman masonry reused in the present building and a thirteenth-century chapel that is obscured by fourteenth-century side chapels. The tower and nave are fifteenth century with a magnificent, sixteenth-century panelled ceiling to the nave. The oak roof bosses are embellished with foliage and feature grotesque

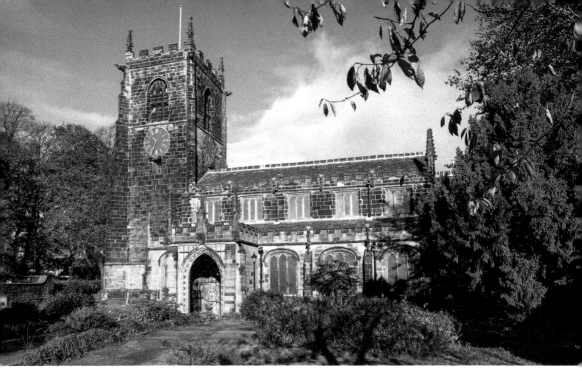

Above: All Hallows from the south.

Right: All Hallows' nave looking east.

faces, tools of the passion, the sun, moon and more. It is also charmingly inscribed 'Geferay Doyson was the Maker of this MCCCCCXXII'.

Restorations and alterations of the 1870s by architect W. H. Crossland were extensive but not brutal. Many windows, furnishings and monuments survived and often delight, such as the 10-feet-high painted and gilded font cover.

A 1990 octagonal square-roofed controversial extension *à la* Wakefield Cathedral's 1982 chapter house, designed by Peter Marshall of York, was built in sandstone to the north side of the church. The £225,000 hall and facilities are separate from the church but connected to the nave by a reopened doorway and lobby.

Listed grade I
See also Crossland 18, 25, 27 & 31

3. Finthorpe Grange Barn, Finthorpe Lane

Formerly Thorpe House Farm barn, it is an example of a now rare local building type. It is said to be the largest and finest cruck framed barn in the county. Dating from the late sixteenth century, it is built of thin rubble stone. It has a pitched stone-flagged roof supported on six cruck trusses that give a clear height of 24 feet across five bays.

Cruck trusses, pairs of massive curved timber posts, were the earliest manner of supporting a roof on a rectangular stone building where the timbers reach from the wall base to the roof's apex. Each truss is stabilised with tie beams and to each other with beams at wall top and apex. The crucks are of timber from trees felled around 1595.

To the north side, facing the road, an aisle was added in the seventeenth century. It has a gabled cart entrance with double doors and later roof lights. The barn became Corporation property on the purchase of the Ramsden estate and was let until 1991. It was listed in 1952 but in 1996 the council resolved to sell it in dilapidation. In private hands it has been restored and cared for.

Listed grade II*

Finthorpe Grange Barn from the north, 1952.

Upper portion of cruck trusses at the east end of Finthorpe Grange Barn.

Finthorpe Grange Barn from the north-east.

4. Weavers' Factories, Nos 1 and 3 Fernside Avenue

These three-storey cottages are examples of the local domestic vernacular style developed for industrial use.

Possibly dating from the seventeenth century, they used to be in rural isolation yet had close access to the former road between Almondbury and Huddersfield. The associated barns give an indication of the mixed economy of such households described by Defoe in his *Tour Through the Whole of the Island of Great Britain*.

One has an eight-light stone mullioned range with glazing bars on first and second floors, the other with a six-light mullioned range. Both had five-light stone mullioned windows on the ground floor. Alterations include an extra window and a blind window.

The weaver's working hours would have been limited by the length of daylight. The long rows of south-facing windows gave light to loom shops of the home-working weaver, with living quarters on the ground floor. With the development of powered mills such domestic industry became less significant in the nineteenth century.

By 1920 the properties were part of the Ramsden estate, so on the estate's purchase by Huddersfield Corporation, it became part of the 'miscellaneous' housing stock, which was ill-maintained. In the 1950s the area was developed with council houses. They two cottages are now privately owned.

Listed grade II

Above: Fernside Avenue.

Left: Weaver's factory, Fernside Avenue, 1975.

5. Market Cross, Market Place

In 1671 John Ramsden, owner of the Manor of Huddersfield, applied to the Crown to hold a market in Huddersfield. Charles II, after a local enquiry on 12 September where twelve 'good and honest men' attested that it would not prejudice the king or others, granted the right to hold a weekly market in the town on 1 November. This franchise gave Ramsden the monopolistic market franchise for a radius of 6 2/3 miles and allowed the collection of market tolls.

The stone market cross must have been first erected soon after 1671. It has strong authoritarian symbolism with the orb of the monarch supreme above a square die with arms of Ramsden marriages, supported by a column with an ionic capital (symbolic of rams horns) above the tiers of the common people.

Parts of the cross and its base have been replaced over the years – at one time the die was of concrete and the orb of iron. It has been painted several times, taken down, broken up, restored and re-erected many times in the square, and removed by 1812 for fear of it being a centre of action by radicals. On its return in 1851 a newspaper letter referred to it as a 'mutilated remnant of the past', 'unsightly and unmeaning'.

In 1806 a man sold his wife for half a guinea (52.5p) at the cross. It has also been the platform for political rallies, women's suffrage, preachers, pacifists, army recruitment, war memorialisation, trade union meetings, rag stunts, protests and more.

> Countless are the feet that have trodden on its pavement; unnumbered and unwritten are the life stories of most people who have gazed on the straight stone pillar which is there, or sat on its broad base.

Above left: Market Cross.

Above right: Market Cross detail.

Right: *Market Place, 1965*, by Harold Blackburn. Waverley Chambers is to the right.

Joy at its sweetest, and sorrow at it bitterest moment – happiness, comedy, tragedy – these are some of those life's certainties that have known this spot as their birthplace, whereby they have served to form those links of remembrance that death only could sever.

Huddersfield Examiner, 1 July 1911

6. Cloth Hall Shelter and Gateway, Ravensknowle Park

Set in the park is a pavilion that started out in a very different manner in the town centre.

Huddersfield Cloth Hall was built off what is now Half Moon Street for Sir John Ramsden, 3rd Baronet. Building began in March 1765 and it opened in November 1766. The exterior of the massive brick-built oval building was grim and secure, without perimeter windows but with a fine symmetrical main entrance lodge that had a central projecting pedimented bay – all dressed with stone quoins

Cloth Hall Pavilion, Ravensknowle Park.

Former Cloth Hall entrance from Ravensknowle Road.

and surmounted by a clock tower, lantern campanile and cupola – rather more 'Oxbridge' college than Huddersfield (Ramsden was a fellow commoner of Clare College, Cambridge).

The hall was to be the trading place for cloth pieces – the output of the clothiers with handlooms. Cobbett visited the morning after his Water Works speech; the *Yorkshire Gazette* reported 'his reception there was cold, and in one case insulting'.

Extensive industrialisation and the railways were to limit its life but the building was significant for a century. It was enlarged and extended in 1780, 1848 and again in 1864 but then soon fell into decline.

In 1881 the ground floor became an exchange and newsroom. There was also a Chamber of Commerce council chamber and a members' reading room. That all closed on 31 December 1929 and the building was cleared away by August 1930. In 1934 consent was given for the Market Street site to be developed as the Ritz/ ABC cinema of 1936–83. The site is now a Sainsbury's and Specsavers.

Fragments of the Cloth Hall were retained by the Corporation and reassembled in 1931 as the pavilion. Arched openings, ten interior Tuscan columns, the clock and cupola and brickwork were engineered into a unique shelter. Two commemorative plaques from the hall were remounted.

In 1932 the Cloth Hall's magnificent Gibbs surround entrance of 1780 that had been on Sergeantson Street was erected as a gateway in the park. It remains in place but is now a privately owned feature between Nos 139 and 141 Ravensknowle Road.

Listed grade II
See also Cobbett 10–11

7. Sir John Ramsden Court, Wakefield Road

Although it had been anticipated by others, in the early 1770s Sir John Ramsden, who owned almost all of Huddersfield, saw that a canal linking the town to the navigable River Calder at Cooper Bridge around 3 miles away was in his interest. A 1774 Parliamentary Act authorised Sir John to make and maintain a navigable canal.

Canal warehouse, Aspley, 1972, from the east.

Above: Canal warehouse, Aspley, 1973, from the north.

Left: Sir John Ramsden Court from the south.

The canal's opening in 1776, with a canal basin and wharfs at Aspley, changed the town's fortunes. The transport of coal, timber, bricks, wool and machinery was made possible. To make such commerce, efficient warehouses were erected at Aspley, of which only two remain.

One of them was built for Sir John by a wharf off Wakefield Road and on the canal side. It was described in a 1778 estate survey as the new woollen warehouse.

It's a handsome industrial building of three storeys with an attic, built in coursed hammered stone with massive quoins and a stone slate roof. It had four getting-in doors to the canal and towards the road a projecting gabled bay with four getting-in doors. There are ranges of multi-mullioned windows. In the attic of the north-west gable is a Venetian window – rather a surprise.

It is probably the oldest intact building in the town centre and may be the only one of its type in the country. For a while known as Atkinson's warehouse, the first 200 years of its use is obscure but it survived the end of the canal age, the loss of the wharf and dereliction in the 1970s, when all around was cleared. It has had many alterations including a two-storey extension of between 1780 and 1825, which has been truncated by road widening and the whole partially obscured by Wakefield Road being raised.

The building was saved by listing in 1973 and later Marino Bevilacqua converted it into flats. The process saved the building but it was not sympathetic; externally the porch makes a nonsense of the building's design. By 2015 the University of Huddersfield bought the whole building and AHR converted it into offices, mitigating the 1980s damage and use of modern materials.

Listed grade II*
See also AHR 1, 30, 38, 44, 46 & 50; Bevilacqua 36

8. Cloth Hall Chambers, Cloth Hall Street

Yards are not peculiar to Huddersfield yet the late eighteenth-century town developed many scores of such enclosed spaces as the yard was the affordable development style, with properties on relatively planned streets having higher rents. Huddersfield's yards have histories of residential, artisan, commercial, stabling, warehousing and industrial use. Many were associated with overcrowding and insanitary conditions, some were gentrified into arcades and shopping malls, most were lost in redevelopment.

This is an example of a commercial yard. There was a cart passage through the right side of No. 12 until 1913 when electrician Guy Laycock converted the street-fronting building into a shop. Since then the yard has been accessed only on foot between Nos 12 and 14 Cloth Hall Street. Upper-floor rooms are reached by stone steps and iron balconies. It has been previously known as Tinner's Yard (by 1822), Lancaster's Yard (possibly after the water commissioner, auctioneer and property owner John Lancaster, who died in 1855 (1850s–1913) and Laycock's Yard (1913–24).

Below left: Cloth Hall Chambers from the south-west.

Below right: Cloth Hall Chambers from the south-east.

The earliest occupiers over the three floors were mostly fancy woollen manufacturers, merchants and agents – thirty-two had addresses here in 1822. There has since been a great diversity of commercial uses.

Unlisted

9. Lawrence Batley Theatre, Queen Street

When John Wesley first preached in Huddersfield in 1757 he described his impression of the inhabitants: 'A wilder people I never saw in England'. This inauspicious start of his evangelism in the town was overcome. He preached again from the market cross in 1772 and the first Methodist chapel was built off what is now Chapel Hill in 1775. A split in 1796, when the New Connexion movement took control of the chapel, led to Wesleyan Methodists looking for a new home. They leased a Ramsden-owned plot off the lower corner of King Street and Queen Street in 1798 and built a chapel there, opening in 1800.

As chapel membership flourished, there was need for a larger building. In 1818 Joseph Kaye was awarded the masonry contract for the new chapel along Queen Street. The architects are thought to have been Charles Watson and James Piggott Pritchett of York.

This chapel opened in 1819 and was 'one of the most handsome and commodious chapels in the kingdom', holding 3,000 people. It was described in 1822 as the 'largest Methodist Chapel in the Kingdom' and said to hold 2,400. It was big. The crypt had space for over 1,000 burials.

There were many years of chapel life with membership growth and more buildings. In 1906 it had a new role as a mission with a strong social work record and a Women's Home, and then decline. Demolition and commercial redevelopment was proposed and opposed in 1963. The Mission moved to new premises on King Street in 1970 and the eighty-four burials of 1819–55 were exhumed.

From 1972 to 1975 the former chapel was a civic arts centre and in 1978 it opened as The Ridings, a squash club with crypt bar and disco. Each new use

Interior of Queen Street Chapel shortly before closing in 1970.

Above: Lawrence Batley Theatre from Queen Street.

Right: Lawrence Batley Theatre from the stage.

brought massive loss to the interior. From 1986 the building was disused and derelict. After twelve years of campaigning for theatre facilities in Huddersfield, the Kirklees Theatre Trust rescued the shell. The 1992–94 £5.3 million redevelopment by Kirklees Council's Design Practice and John Laing Construction gave the town the 477-seat Lawrence Batley Theatre, 150-seat Syngenta Cellar Theatre, rehearsal rooms, bars and a coffee shop. Enjoy.

Listed grade II & II*
See also Kaye 10–13 & 17–18; Pritchett 13, 17, 19 & 20

10. Fire Proof Mill, St Thomas's Road

Joseph Kaye was a major Huddersfield entrepreneur and builder in the first half of the nineteenth century. As a factory proprietor he leased land in 1825 at Folly Hall, which had a working classical six-storey '40 horse' [power] mill by 1827. In ashlar, with pediments to the staircase bays and central pediment over a Venetian window, 'Kaye's factory' is impressive. It was here that William Cobbett was denied a platform in 1830.

Adjoining land was leased and mills were built over 3 acres. Fire in June 1844 burnt out the '40 horse' mill, damaging others – 'the flames were issuing through the roof to a fearful altitude, and through nearly every window in the mill – about 240 in number, in awful grandeur'; 'and burnt from the three upper rows of windows with an awful glare, so that at the distance of a mile the smallest type might have been read distinctly'. The loss to Kaye and his tenants was great. As soon as the site was cold work began with the aim of reopening in January.

The mill was rebuilt in the same style, with fireproof brick vaulting. The '60 horse mill' became known as the 'Fire Proof Mill'.

In 1847 George S Phillips wrote, 'At the foot of my garden runs the canal and a few yards beyond it the river, to the left stand the factories of Joseph Kaye like so many Aladdin palaces with their hundreds of windows and tall steeple chimneys.' Reports of working conditions, accidents and crime give less palatial impressions of the site.

Worsted spinner Joseph Lumb, a tenant from 1853, bought a mill in 1872. Eventually Joseph Lumb & Sons controlled the whole site. A 1979 replacement of some buildings did not prevent Lumb's site closure in 1982, and the mill was deserted by 1993. In 1994 many buildings were cleared for development and car parking. Theft, damage and dereliction followed. It was not until 2008 that work started on rescuing it from complete loss. It is now occupied by an NHS Foundation Trust and the insurers LV.

Listed grade II*
See also Cobbett 6 & 11; Kaye 9, 11–13 & 17–18

Folly Hall Mill burnt out.
(*Illustrated London News*, 8 June 1844)

Above: Folly Hall Mills, with Fire Proof Mill to the right.

Right: Attic floor of Fire Proof Mill, 2009.

11. Water Works Offices, Water Street

At the top of Spring Street is an elegant ashlar façade. Below its pediment is an oval tablet that bears the inscription 'Water Works, Established by Subscription. MDCCCXXIII'. It is all that remains of this enterprise, which was the start of the modern water supply of Huddersfield. Previously water was raised and piped by waterwheel to here from the river at Folly Hall.

'An act for Supplying with Water the Town and Neighbourhood of Huddersfield … gained Royal assent 14 June 1827'. It identified 120 commissioners who were empowered to construct works to supply 'a more ample supply of water of a more pure and salubrious quality'.

The engineer for the waterworks project was Nicolas Brown, who had worked on the construction of Huddersfield Narrow Canal from 1797 until his dismissal in 1801. He was probably the architect of the offices as well. In 1964 John Betjeman described the building as charming and thought Joseph Kaye was 'probably responsible'; however Kaye, who was a water commissioner, was probably the builder.

On 19 January 1830 William Cobbett arrived in the town. Joseph Kaye had given consent for him to give a speech on the top floor of his Folly Hall Mill but under pressure from tenants Kaye he changed his mind. The Huddersfield Shipping Company warehouse, the Court of Requests and The George Inn all refused his supporters. Somebody had keys to the Commissioners' meeting room and Cobbett gave his speech there to 'less than 200'.

The new Huddersfield Corporation bought the works in 1869 for £58,664. Years later the offices became redundant and were used as housing. By 1978 the building was in poor condition, but Kirklees Council's proposal to demolish led to it being listed. In 1981 the district was made a conservation area and a

Water Works plaque of 1828.

Former Water Works offices, 1981.

Former Water Works offices, now rebuilt as housing.

housing action area. In 1983 there was a successful council planning application for retention of the façade with rebuilding to form eight flats. Works supported by English Heritage and West Yorkshire County Council led in 1991 to Kirklees Council being awarded a Diploma of Merit by Europa Nostra and being the winner of the Housing Estate Environmental Improvement category of the Local Government News 'Street Design' competition.

Listed grade II
See also Cobbett 6 & 10; Kaye 9–10, 12–13 & 17–18

12. Former Royal Infirmary, New North Road

Funded through subscriptions, a town centre dispensary was established in 1814 with its object being 'the relief of the industrious poor of the town and district'. It had no provision for inpatients, so treatment was at the dispensary and at home. By 1824 there was pressure for a hospital 'for the Reception of a limited Number of In-Patients more especially for those frequent Accidents arising from the extensive use of Machinery'.

A 2-acre site leased from Sir John Ramsden, much fundraising and a design competition won by architect John Oates led to the 1829 laying of the first stone of the Huddersfield and Upper Agbrigg Infirmary. The main contractor was Joseph Kaye.

The £7,500 ashlar building was magnificent with a giant Greek Doric (a suitable style given that the Ancient Greeks are seen as the fathers of medicine) portico dominating the façade. On opening in 1831 it had twenty beds and the dispensary with an outpatients' consulting room.

The infirmary developed with public support and endowments of cots, beds, wards and wings. A south wing designed by William Cocking opened in 1861, a north wing by John Kirk in 1874. In 1877 medical baths designed by Edward Hughes opened. In 1896 more baths, a laundry and a plant were completed by Ben Stocks, who then redeveloped the south wing.

In 1911 it became the Royal Infirmary, following fundraising for the endowment of the King Edward VII Ward. The funds also paid for the bronze statue of the late king by Bryant Baker, to the front of the building, disdainfully unveiled by George V in 1912. War memorial fundraising paid for more development until control passed from local to public ownership in 1948.

The hospital moved to Lindley in 1965. Huddersfield Corporation bought the hospital site from the Department of Health. Conversion for Ramsden Technical College, which had been on Queen Street South, gave 70,000 square feet of space by September 1968. It became Huddersfield Technical College in 1971. Renamed Kirklees College in 2008, it moved to a new campus in 2013. At the time of writing Trinity One LLP had a planning application that includes partial demolition of the hospital building and alterations for conversion to offices.

Listed grade II*
See also Cocking 15, 21 & 26; Hughes 13, 28, 30, 32, 34 & 48; Kaye 9–11, 13 & 17–18; Kirk 36; Stocks 26 & 29

Kirklees College with Edward VII statue, 2003.

Huddersfield Infirmary.
(Nathaniel Whittock, engraved
by John Shury, 1831)

Former Kirklees College, 2012.

13. St Peter's, Byram Street

Huddersfield parish church, mother of the local Anglian churches, is the third church on this site. The first is said to have been founded in 1073. It was said to be very small, plain and with a spire. It was replaced around 1506 with a new church with a tower. This fell into disrepair by 1830 and in 1834 was entirely demolished for the present church of 1836.

The architect for the new church was J. P. Pritchett. An experienced church builder, William Exley of York, laid reused stone in a manner that saw it crumble even before completion. In 1859 the church was said to have a 'gingerbread appearance' that 'threatens speedily to fall into decay' and it has threatened to do so ever since. Later additions include octagonal vestries flanking the chancel by Pritchett by 1851 and by Edward Hughes in 1879.

By 1841 the church's graveyard was full. There were complaints about the stench and disgusting scenes at every burial. The graveyard was closed to almost all

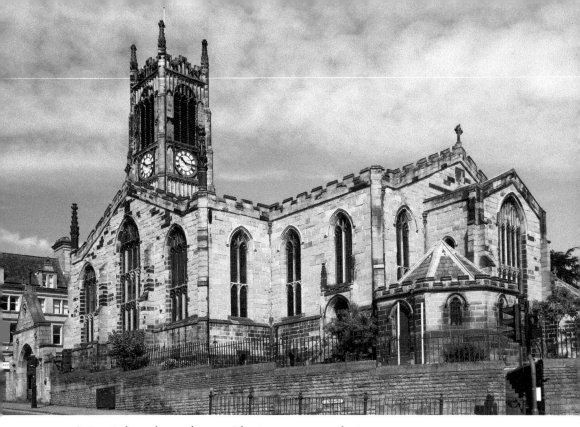

St Peter's from the south-east with 1859 gateway and 1879 vestry.

Above: St Peter's interior from the gallery, looking east.

Left: St Peter's from the north-east with tomb of Joseph Kaye in St Peter's Gardens.

new burials in 1855, levelled in 1858 and cleared in 1952, when the gardens were opened. One of the later burials was of Joseph Kaye, the 'Builder of Huddersfield', in 1858. His table tomb is near the north wall.

The great church architect William Butterfield designed the fine 1859 Gothic archway that faces Cross Church Street.

The white painted interior is rather a surprise with a war memorial east window and classical golden baldachino of 1923, both by another great church architect, Ninian Comper. The panelled ceiling delights with carved and decorated vines. Three galleries enclose the nave to bring an intimacy within the volume of the church.

The church was reordered in the late 1980s, and part of the vaulted crypt is an independent restaurant. Masonry and decorations have been sympathetically restored in recent years under the guidance of local architects One17. In 2017 the church got planning consent for One17's modest reordering with a new entrance lobby, lift, improved crypt community space, conveniences and car park requiring the relocation of Kaye's tomb.

Listed grade II*
See also Hughes 12, 28, 30, 32, 34 & 48; Kaye 9-12 & 17–18; One17; Pritchett 9, 17, 19 & 20

14 Hall of Science, No. 9 Bath Street

The foundation stone of this plain classical building was laid on 2 April 1839 with a resolution that the building was to be

> an Institution sacred to the Truth without mystery, mixture of error or the fear of man – an Institution wherein the principles of a mild and benevolent philosophy shall be exhibited, calculated to bring peace on earth and good will towards men.

It was to be a Hall of Science of the Huddersfield Community Society of Rational Religionists, better known as the Owenites, as Robert Owen was the founder of

Ramsey Clay building, formerly the Hall of Science.

Hall of Science's ceiling with Grists' travelling hoist to a loading door.

the movement. They were socialists that organised events on chapel lines with Sunday 'social services', 'social hymns', 'social missionaries' and a band.

The 45 feet by 51 feet hall, with stained-glass windows, a coffered ceiling and a schoolroom seating 200, was opened on 2 November 1839. There were hymns, music and lectures, such as 'Right Application of Science', one sour moment being when John Brindley, the anti-socialist campaigner, made a violent outburst.

Speakers in the coming years included Owen several times, James Rigby of Harmony Hall and Chartist leader Feargus O'Connor. Due to agitation and actions by Brindley, Wesleyans, many employers, Huddersfield Choral Society, local newspapers, the trade depression of the early 1840s and fraud, the Owenites were soon in financial trouble.

In 1847 the building and contents were auctioned. The hall was bought by Frederick Schwann on behalf of Unitarians, who stayed until moving to their new Fitzwilliam St Church in 1854. From 1855 it was a Baptist chapel and Sunday school until their new North Road church opened in 1878. At auction in 1880 it was bought by James Conacher & Sons and was an organ works until 1902. It was acquired by S. S. Beaumont, a Batley cabinetmaker, and by 1910 was a Railway Mission hall until he sold it in 1919; it was promptly resold to the Grist brothers. The Grists were waste merchants and shoddy makers who used it as a warehouse and manufactory until 1963 when it was bought by Ramsay Clay, painter and decorator, who still occupies this remarkable survivor of radical Huddersfield.

Listed grade II
See also Connacher 29

15. Colosseum, Queensgate

Flanking the entrance arch on the ashlar façade are reliefs of two horses cramped in the inset spaces, one cantering, groomed and controlled, the other wild and rearing. Both show damage from the higher parts being hammered off – it's a long story.

The horses are on the front of a riding school built in 1846–47 by William Wallen for a shareholders' company. In 1848 the school hosted circuses and theatrical acts followed. By 1856 it was the Theatre Royal. In 1859 the architect William Cocking built a substantial stage and proscenium arch. It became the New Theatre Royal.

In 1862 the town's volunteer corps bought the building and made it a drill hall and armoury (excepting being a roller skating rink in 1875 and a brief return to drama when another theatre burnt down in 1880). In 1902 when the corps's new hall opened it was sold to a theatre chain that opened the hall as the Armoury Theatre. In 1904 it was rebuilt by architect Willie Cooper as the 1,246-seat Hippodrome variety theatre. Vesta Tilley starred at the 1905 reopening.

Variety ran until the 1926 modernisation, although there also were religious and socialist rallies and Mrs Pankhurst spoke at a 1906 WSPU rally. It reopened as the New Hippodrome and Opera House, closing in 1930. Conversion to the Tudor House Super Cinema followed with the interior in Elizabethan style – plaster timbering, shields and tapestries.

In 1958 it became the Essoldo after it was bought by that chain. Fire destroyed the upper levels of the building in 1967, which were demolished. The truncated

Below left: Hippodrome Variety Theatre with glazed veranda of 1905.

Below right: Cannon Cinema, 1994.

Building work to redevelop Sin into the Colosseum.

building was refurbished and clad externally in slate, causing the relief horses to be brutally damaged to make them less proud and hidden.

It became the Classic in 1972, Cannon in the 1980s and Tudor again in 1995, holding a gay and lesbian festival and showing arthouse film. Sale and closure came in 1998.

New owners removed the cinema interior and exterior slate cladding revealing the damaged horses. From 1999 a series of bars and clubs followed: Rat & Parrot, Livingstones, Club Ché and Sin , which closed in 2011.

The building is being redeveloped as the Colosseum, an entertainment venue.

Unlisted
See also Cocking 12, 21 & 26; Cooper 32, 35 & 37; Wallen 1 & 18

16. Lockwood Viaduct, Meltham Road

It is said to be one of the largest viaducts in the UK and finest in West Yorkshire. It was built in 1846–49 to carry two tracks of the Penistone line for the Huddersfield and Sheffield Junction Railway (which became the Lancashire & Yorkshire Railway in 1847) for 476 yards.

While it was under construction in 1847, George. S. Philips wrote,

> one of the most stupendous structures of ancient or modern times. It bridges the deep yawning valley with is innumerable pillars and tiers of arches and connects on either side with the old hills which have been rendered since the creation. As you look at it from the Holmfirth road, and see it stretch its enormous length of stone before you. The impression is almost irresistible that is the work of demi-gods and giants.

The design was by John Hawkshaw, and the master mason was Kirkheaton-born Job Hirst, who went on to build Ribblehead Viaduct where he was robbed and killed.

The thirty-six arches reach 136 feet in height. Victoria Tower would pass through them (see 1). All except two are semicircular arches spanning 30 feet. The two road-crossing arches are skewed with spans of 42 and 70 feet. It is worth looking up at the masonry above Meltham Road.

It was built with 972,000 cubic feet of sandstone from the Berry Brow cuttings to the south. The structure is in rubble stone with sneck and jump bonding rather than evenly coursed. Construction mishaps led to at least three deaths, and in every case the inquest verdict was 'accidental death'. The line opened to passenger traffic on 1 July 1850.

From 1856 to 1985 Lockwood Cricket Club was at nearby Birks Bottom. Honley batsman Norman Robinson (1838–90) is said to have hit a ball over the viaduct in the course of play. There are reports of cricket balls being thrown over the viaduct by Charles Hirst (c. 1860), Allen Hill, Jack Crossland (twice in 1874 – once while standing in a barrel) and Jack Crum (twice in 1938). Golf professional Sandy Herd used a filed two wood to hit a gutta percha golf ball over in 1897.

Lockwood Viaduct and Cricketers.

Above: Lockwood Viaduct and cricketers from the south.

Right: Lockwood Viaduct, 1952, from the west.

Lockwood Viaduct
from the south.
Victoria Tower would
fit inside an arch.

17. Huddersfield Station, St George's Square

Ian Nairn's words, 'It is more of a palace then a station, a kind of stately home with trains running through it', an apt description of the magnificence of the 416-foot-long station with a Corinthian portico and colonnades with pavilions.

It has been admired since it was built, as in the *Huddersfield Chronicle* in 1850:

> The railway station is one of the most superb structures in the kingdom. I know not which to admire most – its design or its execution. The former is indebted to vivid conception of Mr Pritchett – the latter to the unrivalled abilities of Mr Joseph Kaye. If future ages should enquire for Mr Kaye's mausoleum let them take their stand in front of the station – and look around!

The landowning Ramsden family was at first reluctant to have a station in the town, wishing to protect its canal interests, but came round to see how it could be beneficial. Earl Fitzwilliam, a Ramsden estate trustee, was able to choose his favoured architect J. P. Pritchett, which may have led to the design being reminiscent of his own palatial classical home, Wentworth Woodhouse.

It was built with a single platform in 1846–50 by two rail companies: the Huddersfield & Manchester Railway (which soon became the Lancashire & Yorkshire Railway) and the London & North Western Railway, which had their own ticket offices in the two pavilions and had a joint committee to run the station. The central building had refreshment rooms, a hotel and offices.

The station was extended with an island platform and overall roof in 1886. In 1965 proposals were made by the Building Design Partnership to demolish the station. In 1968 Huddersfield Corporation bought the main station building and platform two from British Railways.

Public houses now occupy the two pavilions. The square to the front has seen many hustings, protests and rallies. It has been the site of trophy cannon from

Huddersfield station.

Bands of Hope demonstration, St George's Square, 1893. 35,000 people attended. Peel statue to the right.

Sebastopol and then statues of two twice-serving prime ministers, formerly Robert Peel and now locally born Harold Wilson.

Listed grade I
See also Kaye 9–13 & 18; Pritchett 9, 13, 19 & 20

Huddersfield station with Ian Walter's 1999 bronze statue of Harold Wilson.

18 George Hotel, St George's Square

In the mid-1840s there was expectation of the railways reaching Huddersfield and it would lead to a station being built to the north-west of the town centre, enabling full commercial development. However, after a tussle of competing interests St George's Square was realised with development around.

To layout John William Street the Ramsden-owned George Hotel on the Market Place would need to be demolished. As the station plans were drawn Ramsden estate agent George Loch realised that the railway companies were considering a great railway hotel in the main station building. The solution was to announce the building of a Ramsden-owned grand hotel so that the railway company directors would drop their own hotel plans and the estate would continue to enjoy the rental income.

Loch asked architect William Wallen for plans, which were ready in early 1849. Builder Joseph Kaye, who had lots of stone on site left over from the station's construction, won the tender. Later that year Loch considered the hotel

George Hotel with a trophy Sebastopol cannon on display, 1858–73.

George Hotel.

George Hotel from Northumberland Street, with station portico beyond.

'the most substantial and best constructed edifice I know anywhere'. It opened on 22 September 1851 and cost £10,770.

The hotel's four storeys to the square are in ashlar with dramatic rustication of the ground floor and vermiculated quoins setting a high design standard for later elevations on the square. The John William Street extension was built in 1854, laundry and kitchens by W. H. Crossland in 1874 and huge extension to the rear in 1899.

In its early days the hotel had an open visitor's book that allowed people to see which buyers and commercial people were in town.

On 29 August 1895 twenty-one Lancashire and Yorkshire rugby clubs held a meeting here over payments for players and voted to secede from the Rugby Football Union to set up the Northern Rugby Football Union. In 1922 this became the Rugby Football League.

The sixty-bedroom hotel closed without warning in January 2013. In April it was bought by dentist and property developer Dr Altaf Hussain, who said he intended to restore and upgrade the building. It remains closed and is for sale.

Listed grade II*
See also Crossland 2, 25, 27 & 31; Kaye 9–13 & 17; Wallen 1 & 15

19. Lion Chambers, John William Street

Samuel Oldfield, woollen manufacturer and railway speculator, had ambition. He had a grand arcade built across the square from the station with a gala opening in January 1854. Around 7,000 people visited on the first day and there was praise: 'It has risen like an exhalation of morning dew, diaphanous and dazzling, the *chef d'oeurve* of our town'.

The arcade was designed by J. P. Pritchett on a Ramsden estate site. It was to be the Royal Arcade but after the installation of an artificial stone lion on the parapet in February 1853 it became Lion Arcade. At 11 feet 6 inches long and 7 tons the lion came by train from London. As the beast was craned up the new building a chain snapped and it fell 7 feet, landing face down. The lion was the work of John Seeley, a medal winner at the Great Exhibition of 1851.

The building had a row of shops with the novelty of large plate glass windows facing the square with more units on the side streets. Above were wool warehouses and below a wool bale cellar. From the street through the central main entrance there was a Crystal Palace-inspired 112 feet by 48 feet central arcade with a clear height of 50 feet to an arched glass or 'splendid crystal' roof. This conservatory had sparkling fountains with goldfish. The gardener Joshua Major offered conservatory plants with garden statuary from Seeley and exotic birds. The twelve shop units in the arcade reused Titus Salt's display fittings from the Great Exhibition. The atrium was lit by 120 gas jets.

Oldfield had over extended himself and was bankrupted in April 1855 but the family bought the arcade back in August.

From 1919 to 1921 attempts were made to redevelop the arcade as a cinema; when that failed perimeter shops extended into the space. It became Lion Chambers.

The lion stood proudly until 1977 but by then it was in a poor state – its fall in 1853 was probably injurious to its concrete blocks' long-term integrity. It was dismantled and replaced by a 4 cwt fibreglass copy. There is an intact and in-situ 'stone' brother lion in The Arboretum, Lincoln.

Listed grade II
See also Major 20; Pritchett 9, 13, 17 & 20

Lion Chambers.

Painting of the 1853 lion. The George Hotel is in the background.

Replica fibreglass lion. It's worn HTFC colours since May 2017.

2c. Edgerton Mortuary Chapels, Cemetery Road

In 1841 St Peter's churchyard was reported by the *Leeds Mercury* to be

> so densely filled with mortal remains that it is found necessary to enlarge it and we are glad to learn there will be little or no difficulty in accomplishing so desirable an object. A public cemetery has been talked of and there are hopes that one of these interesting modern improvements will ere long be established in this populous district.

There were to be fourteen years of frustration and disputes about various rights, location, accessibility and burial fees. In 1849 the Huddersfield Improvement Commissioners took up the issue and eventually reached an agreement with the Ramsden estate's trustees for a site off Blacker Lane.

Proposed Edgerton mortuary chapels (from a sketch by J. P. Pritchett, 1853).

Edgerton mortuary chapels, tower and central avenue.

The Commissioners needed legislation to proceed and limit rights for burial elsewhere. Two public inquiries and four Parliamentary bills later, royal assent was granted for the Huddersfield Burial Ground Act in June 1852 and an amending Act in 1855.

The 12-acre site was passed to the Commissioners in September 1852. Architects Pritchett & Sons designed a pair of mortuary chapels. The Anglican and Nonconformist chapels were to be a cost-saving single structure at the centre of the cemetery joined by an arch, tower, belfry and spire over an avenue. The vicar refused to allow consecrated and unconsecrated chapels to be joined by stone and mortar. The argument split the town. In November 1854 plans were changed, with 12-inch air gaps hidden by buttresses between each chapel and the tower.

The masonry was by Abraham Graham, and the avenues and grounds were laid out and planted by Joshua Major of Leeds.

The Bishop of Ripon consecrated the upper burial area and a chapel in June 1855. The cemetery opened in October with most churches refusing to take part in the other chapel's dedication as a Unitarian minister was involved.

In 1985 Kirklees Council, not wanting to maintain the listed chapels, proposed demolition of one and the arch. Objections prevented the loss. In 2008, having bricked up the chapels' windows and piled up the interiors with rotting tree prunings, the council asked for ideas for reuse. The chapels and arch stand derelict and fenced off.

Listed grade II
See also Graham 1, 21, 25, 32 & 34; Major 19; Pritchett 9, 13, 17 & 19

21. Britannia Buildings, St George's Square

Across the square from the George Hotel, George Crosland & Sons, woollen manufacturers, and merchants of Crosland Moor and Lockwood leased another Ramsden estate site to build Britannia Buildings.

The design of the huge 1859 building developed from the George's style into a magnificent but austere palazzo. It had accentuated rustication and vermiculation, fine masks on the keystones of the ground-floor windows, parapet urns and a huge figure of Britannia with accoutrements. It is disappointing that it was warehousing for the Croslands and tenants.

It was designed by William Cocking and built by Abraham Graham. It was a very powerful statement by George's sons, two of whom became MPs for the town. Eldest son Thomas Pearson was a Liberal, and served from 1865 until his death in 1868. At a hustings in front of the building he asked 'could he, who had known what it was to work, and to work hard, be an enemy to the working man?' Third son, Sir Joseph, serving from 1893 to 1895, was the first and only Conservative returned by the town.

The tenants changed to include the Huddersfield Building Society, which took offices to the rear of the ground floor in 1902, becoming the society's head office in 1908. In 1924 the society bought the building from the Crosland family for £30,000. In 1926 Architect Clifford Hickson introduced a new façade to the

Britannia Buildings showing the 1926 ground-floor façade to St George's Square.

Above left: Britannia Buildings elevation to John William Street.

Above right: Station Street detail of Britannia Buildings.

ground floor, inserting large bronze-framed plate glass windows and neo-Egyptian stonework in homage to Howard Carter's recent discoveries in the Valley of the Kings. His new entrance gave wide access to a marble-lined business hall with marble-faced columns and Corinthian bronzed capitals.

Two remarkable women are associated with the building. Mary Elaine Sykes, one of the first women in England to qualify as a solicitor, opened her own practice here in 1930. In 1937 she was the first female alderman and in 1945 first female mayor of Huddersfield. The 1960 Olympic gold medallist Anita Lonsbrough lived here from 1955, her father being the caretaker.

The building society outgrew the premises, finally leaving in 1994. The ground floor is now a restaurant and a dentist's, and the upper floors are residential.

Listed grade II*
See also Cocking 12, 15 & 26; Crosland 22; Graham 1, 20, 25, 32 & 34; Hickson 41

22. Mechanics Institution, Northumberland Street

The Huddersfield Mechanics Institution developed from a Young Men's Mental Improvement Society that was founded in 1841. It operated from premises on Outcote Bank, New Street and Queen Street until the purpose-built institute opened on Northumberland Street in 1861.

In 1858 woollen merchant Thomas Pearson Crosland bought, at auction, a building plot on the Carr House estate for £1,700 and offered it at cost to the Institution, which was taken up with enthusiasm. The Manchester architects Travis and Mangnall produced the classical three blind-arched design that was built by Jonathan Sutcliffe and Thomas Dearnley. The front has detailing including wreaths and large incised lettering. Carr House, behind, was retained.

Above: The Creative Lofts, Northumberland Street.

Right: Mechanics Institution in dereliction, 1994.

The Earl of Ripon, having witnessed his wife lay the foundation stone in 1859, said he trusted the building 'through many generations will confer benefit upon this town and neighbourhood'. The institute flourished and merged in 1883 with the town's Female Educational Institute and moved in 1884 (*see* 32).

The building was purchased and remodelled as the Huddersfield Friendly and Trades Society Club and hall in 1886, where it remained until closure in 1985.

The buildings were bought by a private speculator who allowed them to fall into dangerous dereliction. In 1999, after much concern and effort by Kirklees Council, People for Places and North British Housing Association, the Bramley architects Brewster Bye got consent for a radical redevelopment that saved the buildings. In February 2002 twenty-one Creative Lofts were completed. Under the management of the adjacent Media Centre they form part of a nascent cultural quarter.

Listed grade II*
See also Crosland 21

23. Nab End Tower, Back Thornhill Road

On the eminence of Nab End is a battered Scottish broch-like lookout. It was completed by 10 August 1861 during Longwood Thump, the local industrial feast.

> It is curious affair. It stands about 20 feet high, and 12 or 15 feet wide at the base. It is entirely solid throughout, being built of dry stones. It has steps running round the outside from bottom to the top, and the top is protected by a parapet several feet high. The tower has been built (under the permission of Wm Shaw Esq, the proprietor of the land) by the working men of the neighbourhood who, having a great deal of idle time on their hands in consequence of the slackness of trade, took it into their heads to build a memorial of their industry and good habits instead of wasting their time and money in the public house. (*Huddersfield Examiner*)

At 6 a.m. on the Thump's Sunday in 1869 a benefit concert of a Handel oratorio was held at the tower, which was attended by 3,000 people. In 1873 a committee was established to organise an annual Nab End Oratorio at 7 a.m. The concerts have been held annually ever since. They are now known as Longwood Sing, 'The Mother of all Sings', and held at 2.30 p.m. on the 2nd Sunday in September.

In 1895 Shaw's grandson gave 8 acres including the tower to the Corporation. He rebuilt the tower by 1898 – not wishing the Corporation to bear the expense.

Nab End Tower from the west. Castle Hill is on the horizon.

Above: Nab End Tower from the east.

Right: Harold Wilson MP (front centre) arriving at the centenary Longwood Sing, 1973.

The tower was much damaged by visitors throwing stones from the top, theft and inherent structural weaknesses. Several dry-stone buttresses have been added.

In 1958 the council planned to demolish the tower but popular opposition led to a rethink and £200 was spent on repairs. Still more repairs were made but cracks appeared. In 2008 the unlisted tower was renovated by the council at a cost of £200,000. This used a Cintec system of stainless steel rods and grouting to stabilise it. The tower was then refaced to disguise the repairs.

The view from the top is wonderful.

Unlisted

24. 1535 The Melting Point

John Haigh & Sons, textile machine builders and ironfounders, was in business by 1835. In 1876 the company erected the Priestroyd ironworks on the corner of Queen Street South and Firth streets. The premises suffered fires in 1877, 1881, 1911 and 1944 but the five-storey building was occupied by the company and its textile trade tenants until the 1970s. The building was listed in March 1977, in October that year the empty building suffered another serious fire.

In 2000 SKA Textiles, the building's owner, was refused permission to demolish the building to use the land as parking. The planning committee took the view that options for the building in order had not been explored.

In early 2002 the pigeon-infested loft was the location for promotional photographs of veteran punk band The Damned. Later that year Lanson

Above left: 1535 The Melting Point from Queen Street South.

Above right: Dave Vanian and Patricia Rainone of The Damned in Priestroyd Mill, 2002.

Developments announced plans to convert the building into fifty-two flats with parking and a restaurant.

In 2005 Huddersfield Civic Society gave Lanson and its architects, Acumen, an award for the completed restoration. It is now known as 1535 The Melting Point. Can a top floor resident claim 'I had The Damned in my attic'?

Listed grade II
See also SKA 44

25. Estate Buildings

Huddersfield's rapid expansion following the opening of the railway and subsequent property development led the Ramsden family to move their estate office from Longley Hall, near Almondbury, to a prominent town centre site close to the station.

The 1868 Incorporation of Huddersfield and its new powers may also have been a factor for the Ramsdens in building such a bold expression of authority. Its site, including the ancient Cherry Tree Inn was ripe for development allowing wide streets and quality buildings – boosting rental income.

The Ramsden's choice of architect was local man William Henry Crossland, who had been a pupil of George Gilbert Scott, with an impressive record including the in-progress Rochdale Town Hall.

Mason Benjamin Graham started work in August 1868 and it opened in September 1870. The huge and stunning Gothic block turns the corner of Westgate and Railway Street dramatically with an elaborately decorated projecting bay with spire and a porch to an intended hotel. On Westgate over shop units was the Huddersfield Club with tourelles and gables above, and on Railway Street were estate offices with a roofline festival of openwork parapets and spires. Inside there is a Minton encaustic tile hallway to a sculptural stone staircase with Irish marble arcading and the town's first passenger lift, which was built by Broadbent (*see 46*).

The exterior carved stonework by Farmer & Brindley rewards scrutiny. Ten of eleven large shields illustrate the Ramsdens and their advantageous marriages heraldically in chronological order. The last shield was blank until 1967 because in 1870 the 5th baronet had three daughters but no son; it was then that the council had the arms of the town carved on it.

There is also a world of natural history in stone to be discovered on the building: passion flower vines, ivy, grape vines, clover, geraniums, lots of birds, a fawn in buttercups, a squirrel and acorn in potentilla leaves, an owl with a mouse, a hare in oak leaves, a rat, a frog on fern leaves, lizards and much more. There are also three naked men, one with a big nose scratching his head, another one gurning and a third mooning!

Listed grade II
See also Crossland 2, 18, 27 & 31; Graham 1, 20-21, 32 & 34

Estate Buildings from Market Street.

Above: Estate Buildings' Railway Street elevation from St George's Square, 10 Jun 1869.

Left: Lion with restored paw and shield on Estate Buildings.

26. Eddisons, High Street

From 1851 William Eddison was an auctioneer and valuer at No 26 High Street. He survived a shocking Penistone railway accident in 1858 but in November 1870 he died aged sixty-nine having been chilled going home from a sale at the Angel Inn, Paddock.

Long-serving staff, his son John, a valuer, and managing clerk Thomas Albert Taylor succeeded to the business as a partnership and swiftly proposed new premises at Nos 4–6. In July 1871 William Cocking's plans got approval and the offices opened 19 October 1872.

The symmetrical façade is gloriously impure Gothic with alternating pink and yellow sandstone voussoirs to the window heads, pink granite columnettes with Romanesque capitals and non-repeating keystone masks like those of fourteen years previously on Britannia Buildings (*see* 21). Parapet lions holding shields of Huddersfield and York top the extravaganza.

Originally there was offices to the left and a small sale room to the right, with a gated central carriage entrance to the yard giving access by trapdoors for items to be hoisted to the large sale room on the first floor. An electric goods hoist came later.

In 1881 Taylor took over the Huddersfield business, continuing as 'Eddison and Taylor', although Eddison, who had interests in Leeds and Nottingham, was bankrupted in 1882. John James Booth joined the firm so it became Eddison, Taylor & Booth – the town's major auction house and estate agency for over a century.

In the 1970s the saleroom moved to an 1897 glazed rear annexe by Ben Stocks.

In 1987 the Leeds Permanent Building Society took advantage of changes brought by the 1986 Building Societies Act by acquiring estate agencies including Eddisons. When the Leeds merged with Halifax Building Society in 1995 Eddisons

Above left: Eddison's Offices, High Street.

Above right: Keystone of Eddison's Offices.

survived the branch rationalisation. A management buyout of the commercial arm followed in 1997. The Halifax closed the High Street building in 2000. Decades worth of auctioneer's copies of marked-up sale catalogues and estate mapping were skipped. Some were salvaged and are with West Yorkshire Archive Service.

Since 2000 the building has been generally dark. Occasionally a tenant takes part of the building to sell goods.

Listed grade II
See also Cocking 12, 15 & 21; Stocks 12 & 29

27 Former Post Office, Northumberland Street

By the early 1860s it was clear that the New Street post office, off the Market Place, was too small. No central site for a purpose-built building was found.

Despite opposition, by 1864 the Ramsden estate proposed building an office to be let on Northumberland Street. The Postmaster General wanted a detached single-storey building with roof lights but that would not have yielded enough rent for the Ramsdens. A central block 78 feet long, 18 feet high, with mezzanine, public office and tall warehouses to either side was the compromise.

The Ramsdens' preferred architect, W. H. Crossland, prepared plans by 1872 and the land deal made in 1873. The council approved the plans in January 1874.

Dugdale Bros tower, part of the 1875 former post office building.

Dugdale Bros warehousing in the former post office business hall (late 1950s).

The robust Gothic post office opened 23 December 1875. The first letter posted was to Huddersfield man Sir Charles Sikes, originator of the Post Office Savings Bank. More space was soon needed. The lower warehouse had been taken by textile merchants until 1897 when the post office took it over.

The post office moved across the street in 1914. Dugdale Bros, the oldest remaining cloth merchant in Huddersfield town centre, bought the whole building. The company still trades from the upper tower. The rest of the building has since been a dance school, Christian Fellowship Centre and music school. It is now student accommodation.

Listed grade II
See also Crossland 2, 18, 25 & 31

28 Spring Grove School, Water Street

By 1878 architect Hughes had designed Beaumont Street and Crosland Moor schools for the Huddersfield School Board when the Ramsden estate offered the elevated site of the Spring Grove mansion estate for a school of 850 children.

The board heard 'the architect should be a man who would be able to make something of it in a picturesque point of view. It was an exceptionally fine situation' and gave Hughes the job without any competition.

In Hughes's radical design, a two-storey hall is enclosed by fourteen classrooms, each for forty pupils. This was an improvement on the pioneering classroom style of the Albert Road Board School in Saltaire. Opened by the education reformer A. J. Mundella MP in 1880, it was visited by many other school boards.

The school has continued with a history of progressive thinking. Thomas Macnamara taught here from 1882 to 1884. In 1896 he became National Union of Teachers president and published his *Schoolmaster Sketches*, stories drawing attention to the difficulties of elementary school teaching, especially in the very poor parts of urban centres. He was a Liberal MP from 1900 to 1924 and Minister of Labour from 1920 to 1922.

Trevor Burgin was appointed headmaster in 1958. By then the area had seen better days:

Above: Hall of Spring Grove School from the ground floor, looking south.

Right: Spring Grove School's south elevation, 1996.

Hall of Spring Grove School from the first floor, looking north.

the school is flanked by rows of decaying, soot covered terraced houses , joined by quiet cobbled streets ... Nowadays the buildings are obviously dying, occasionally rat-infested. Many are destined for slum clearance, and many more house large numbers of immigrant families. (Burgin & Edson)

It was the first school in England to have more than half the pupils the children of Commonwealth immigrants. In 1967 Burgin co-wrote a book with staff member Paddy Edson, *Spring Grove: The Education of Immigrant Children*, which outlined the pioneering work integrating the pupils into mainstream education and teaching English as a second language. Burgin led the first party of British educationalists to the Punjab and in 1972 was awarded an OBE for his contribution to multiracial education.

In 2011 head teacher Hawa Bibi Laher was awarded an OBE for services to education.

Unlisted
See also Hughes 12, 13, 30, 32, 34 & 48

29 Huddersfield Town Hall, Corporation Street

Huddersfield became a municipal borough on incorporation in 1868. The Corporation's councillors and aldermen met in the Philosophical Hall, which stood where the Piazza's grass is, while its offices were on the site of Lidl on Castlegate. The expense, site and development of a new hall were contentious – a low-cost site was leased from the Ramsden estate and has led to criticism ever since.

I found almost every other building, public and private, before I came upon the head-centre of the Huddersfield Corporation round the corner of a back street. And as I gazed I wondered – wondered what excess of modesty had prompted the Corporation to bestow upon themselves so 'far from the madding crowd' – wondered at the singular architectural effect of the disjointed stonework which stood before me – wondered why the building should have been built in two halves ... (*Huddersfield Chronicle*, 1 April 1882)

The project started with the building of the two-storey 1875–78 Italianate municipal offices, tight to Ramsden Street, Corporation Street and Peel Street. The borough surveyor, John Henry Abbey, was tasked to provide much on a small budget with the possibility of the building being turned into a warehouse should the building become redundant. Eventually, with the council chamber, mayor's reception room and other offices expensively appointed, costs rose to over £19,000.

The day the offices were opened the foundation stone for the town hall was laid. This much taller two-storey building reaching Princess Street is an extension of the dwarfed offices. Also designed by Abbey, it included a large galleried public hall and the borough magistrates' court. The free classical design is rather more celebratory than the restrained offices but again without civic space.

Abbey died aged forty-nine in 1880. The building was completed under the supervision of Ben Stocks. The cost was estimated to be £25,000 but was actually £60,000. It opened with a musical festival in October 1881.

Town Hall's municipal offices from Victoria Lane.

Town Hall's concert hall and court from Princess Street.

Town Hall's concert hall from balcony.

The hall's interior is glorious. Local choirs and others had been campaigning for years for a concert hall and here was a splendid space. It seated 2,250 people (now 1,200). The organ by Henry Willis & Sons was purchased from Newport's Albert Hall and rebuilt by Huddersfield's James Connacher & Sons.

The keystones of the hall's windows are busts of classical gods, all of which can be identified with cheat sheets. Outside on Princess Street the keystones show Sir Matthew Hale, George Frederic Handel, William Hogarth, Sir Isaac Newton, William Shakespeare and James Watt with symbols of their professions.

Listed grade I
See also Connacher 14; Stocks 12 & 26

30 Albert Hotel, Victoria Lane

This remarkable corner public house of 1879 was designed in a Tudor Gothic style by Edward Hughes to replace the Albert Hotel on New Street, which was converted to a printing works.

The building's complicated corner design may be unique. Other features include the heavy glazing bars and an imp on the parapet.

The ground floor's interior has been repeatedly refurbished. A 1970 £10,000 reordering by Abbey and Hanson Rowe closed the off-sales office, reused stained

Above left: Albert Hotel.

Above right: Imp on the parapet of the Albert Hotel, 2018.

glass and privacy screens, retained curved marble topped bars and bar-screen bearing the Wildean epigram 'WORK IS THE CURSE OF THE DRINKING CLASSES'.

The pub has a long association with politicians and the *Huddersfield Daily Examiner*. Huddersfield Town Football Club was founded at a meeting here, hosted by the landlord William Hardcastle on 25 June 1908. Hardcastle, a founding director, became chairman in 1913 but retired early 1914. In October 1919 the proposal to transfer the club to Leeds to take the place of the defunct Leeds City led Hardcastle to inaugurate and host the 'Retention Committee' at the Albert. The Huddersfield club was saved. The Albert has been the meeting place of many campaigning, political and social groups including the Albert Poets founded in 1993.

Unlisted
See also A&HR 1, 7, 38, 44, 46 & 50; Hughes 12, 13, 28, 32, 34 & 48

31. Kirkgate Buildings, Byram Street

The Ramsdens' Victorian development of the town climaxed with the opening of Waverley Buildings, Kirkgate Buildings and Somerset Buildings in 1882–85. The three commercial blocks on Kirkgate, Church Street and Byram Street, costing over £44,000, were a substantial and prestigious development replacing squalid yards. They were also the last works commissioned by the Ramsdens from their star architect W. H. Crossland, who was also working on his masterpiece Holloway College at Virginia Water.

The projects are not unrelated in style. Not Gothic, but a Queen Anne/French/ Flemish embellishment of commercial utility. The rooflines show highly decorated dormers, pinnacles and spires.

The Italian sculptor Ceccardo Egidio Fucigna had worked on Crossland's former master, G. G. Scott Albert memorial. Crossland engaged Fucigna to work at Holloway College, which led to him to also design and execute some of the remarkable stone carvings here. There are Ramsden and industry references and also Greek deities, fabulous beasts, birds and more.

Waverley opened as a temperance hotel with shops below. Somerset became the town's first public library and art gallery with shops below and Kirkgate as a massive first floor office and warehouse arcade with shops below. In 1891 A. J. Balfour opened the Huddersfield and County Conservative Club, which took much of the arcade until 1986.

Kirkgate Buildings, with Waverley Chambers to the left. (*The Builder*, 1883)

Neaverson, No. 4 Byram Street.

Kirkgate Buildings from Kirkgate. Waverley Chambers is to the left.

In 1935 the china and glass dealer Neaverson took a ground-floor lease where Sharp and Law of Bradford refitted and put in new fronts to No. 7 Wood Street and No. 4 Byram Street, which was 'as ingenious as a music-hall illusionist's apparatus' – it still impresses with its reflection killing windows. Inside, the streamlined shop fittings of oak were sprayed silver in the lower showroom and gold in the upper. The shop closed in 2007. The fronts and fittings are in place as the Zephyr Bar & Kitchen.

By the 1970s the arcade was shabby with ill-thought alterations. In 1985 the council was told that £750,000 was need for repair and upgrade for reletting. In 1993 after two years work and £1.5 million it reopened as council offices.

Listed grade II
See also Crossland 2, 18, 25 & 27

32. Ramsden Building, Queensgate

The front half of this three-storey Gothic delight was paid for with subscriptions of members and philanthropic supporters, to house the Technical School & Mechanics' Institution through a merger with the town's Female Educational Institute. It opened in July 1883 with a six-month Fine Art and Industrial

Above: Ramsden Building.

Left: Ramsden Building's first-floor war memorial.

Exhibition, which had 229,000 visitors and raised funds offsetting the £20,000 cost of the building.

Designed by the architect Hughes and built by Benjamin Graham, it had cloth manufacture, dyeing and chemistry laboratories and workshops as well as lecture halls and classrooms for science, arts, languages and commerce. The need for the planned extension was soon apparent. This came in 1901, and was designed by Willie Cooper and built at a cost of £32,000 and two men's lives.

The college and institution became Huddersfield Technical College in 1896. The college continued to expand into other new buildings. In 1958 it was renamed Huddersfield College of Technology from which Ramsden Technical College was split in 1963. When the latter moved out in 1968 the College of Technology took over the whole building. Two years later a merger with Huddersfield Oastler College formed Huddersfield Polytechnic, which became the University of Huddersfield in 1992. The building now houses the university's School of Human and Health Sciences.

The building's front has four lions holding shields that bear the coats of arms of the Worshipful Company of Clothworkers, Huddersfield Corporation, Sir John William Ramsden, landowner, and Sir Thomas Brooke, last president of the Mechanics' Institution, first president of the Technical School and Mechanics' Institute and chairman of Huddersfield Chamber of Commerce.

On the first-floor landing is an allegorical triptych called *Victory* in memory of Technical College students and staff who fought and fell in 1914–18. The three canvases portraying war, peace and death are in a massive art deco oak mount including a relief cenotaph with a bronze plaque. The memorial was unveiled by Sir William Raynor on 19 September 1924. It was largely the work of college staff and students. The painting is by John Richardson Gauld, woodwork by E. Bower and the plaque's modelling by E. Lockwood.

Listed grade II
See also Cooper 15, 35 & 37; Graham 1, 20–21, 25 & 34; Hughes 12, 13, 28, 34 & 48

33. St George's Warehouse, New North Parade

The joint London & North Western Railway and Lancashire & Yorkshire Railway five-storey goods warehouse to the west of the station is impressive in red, blue and buff brick. Costing over £100,000, it was said to be the largest in the country at completion in 1885. It was designed to take massive loading; the walls are over 3 feet thick with the unpartitioned floors being supported by 5,000 tons of iron including fifty-six stanchions resting on stone blocks 7 feet square.

There was criticism by the *Huddersfield Chronicle* as it was being built: 'Not only is it being built of brick, but the most hideous-looking window frames add to its dismal appearance, both combining to make it incongruous with everything surrounding.'

Seven rail lines ran into the ground floor and it had a hydraulic hoist, the frame of which can be seen from platform eight, to raise waggons to the second floor where they could be slid on a traverser across six rail tracks. With systems of capstans, cranes, weighing machines, trap-doors and lifts, goods were processed around the building.

By 1979 the building was disused. Several owners and economic cycles later it remains a sleeping giant.

Listed grade II

Above: St George's Warehouse. The Doric-columned hoist frame is at the corner.

Below: St George's Warehouse's fifth floor, 2008. Cruciform iron stanchions carry timber trusses.

34. Open Market, Brook Street

Huddersfield Corporation acquired the market rights from the Ramsden family in 1876. Edward Hughes designed the Corporation's 1880 Market Hall on King Street. It was both a retail and wholesale market, but the third of the basement allocated to wholesale was found to be inadequate and the roads around too narrow. Traders complained about these and other matters and in 1885 the Corporation resolved to find a site for a new market. In 1886 a site on Zetland Street was promising, however Isaac Horden, cashier of the Ramsden estate, offered this site behind the post office that was twice the area and near the station, tram terminus and town centre with three wide streets. The cost was £5,700 of Corporation stock, and this offer was accepted.

The borough surveyor R. S. Dugdale's design for a fruit, vegetable, flower, fish and game market was an iron frame with glazed walls and a slate six-ridge roof with north light. The plans were adopted in February 1887, Benjamin Graham started groundwork in October and the market opened in August 1888.

The 2,650 square feet roof and thirty-four supporting cast-iron columns up to 30 feet tall were supplied by the Whessoe Foundry, Darlington, at a cost of £3,555. The functional frame was decorated with exotic capitals, an eaves frieze and armorial bearings. The hall, with an auction room, was wooden floored with two avenues serving thirty-two stands and a stone-flagged floor for the eight fish stands.

The market buildings were not erected until the 1920s. Previously there was a wooden building that had been a roller skating rink and from 1911 the Theatre de Luxe Cinema.

Open market, corner of Lord Street and Brook Street.

Above: Open market interior.

Left: Ironwork detail of open market, Byram Street.

In 1973 the Corporation agreed in principle to selling the site for redevelopment. The Huddersfield Society of Architects promptly applied for it to be listed, and although the Corporation objected, it was listed.

The market moved to Red Doles Lane in 1979. In 1980 the listing was upgraded to II*. Reluctantly the Council converted it to a retail, flea and specialist market. A Civic Trust commendation followed in 1983. In 2008 it was given a glamorous repainting emphasising its decorative nature.

See also Graham 1, 20–21, 25 & 32; Hughes 12, 13, 28, 30, 32 & 48

35. Revolución de Cuba, Cross Church Street

The Sun Inn was established as a free house with a modest three-storey frontage on Cross Church Street around 1803, and it offered refreshments and accommodation. To its right there was access to its large livery yard behind, which extended to what became Venn Street and was used for stabling, events and livestock auctions.

Seth Snr was a Shepley stonemason, farmer, publican, colliery owner and brewer. He is reputed to have begun brewing in 1829 after being loaned a sovereign. His home became the Sovereign Inn and the brewery became Seth Senior & Sons at Shepley.

The brewery bought the Sun and two neighbouring shops at an 1887 auction and commissioned architect Willie Cooper and Shepley builder Harris Wood to redevelop the site. The 1890 building application was for a flagship public house, brewery order office, vintners and stores. In 1888–89 Cooper and Wood had built The Cliffe, a large house (now Cliffe House) for the late Seth's fifth son, James.

The street frontage of the 1892 three-storey Sun Buildings was full of drama in ashlar at a cost of £8,000. Stylised shopfronts either side of the gates to the yard, pilasters above and high above a central turret with ogee cupola. To each side massive Queen Anne gables with suns rising and setting and a 1829 George IV sovereign.

Below left: Sun Inn from the north-west, late nineteeth century.

Below right: Sun Inn from the south-west, 1994.

Sun Inn from the north-west.

In 1946 Seth Senior & Sons were bought by Hammonds United Breweries. The Sun Inn kept its name until the 1960s and remained a pub with a magnificent entrance as The Minstrel, Isaacs, Bam and Herbert's on closure in 2016. The order office soon became an auction house and later SR Drapers, Vanity Save, Breads and a Forget Me Not Children's Hospice shop before closure in 2016. Almost all the yard was swallowed up into the 2002 Kingsgate Centre.

After an investment, said to be £1 million, it reopened as the 6,000 square feet Revolución de Cuba bar and restaurant in November 2018.

Unlisted
See also Cooper 15, 32 & 37

36. Trafalgar Mills, Leeds Road

Learoyd Bros & Co. was a substantial Milnsbridge-based woollen and worsted manufacturer when director Albert Ernest Learoyd conceived a model mill. It was built on an open flat site as a 'country mansion' set in gardens with an

Trafalgar Mills.

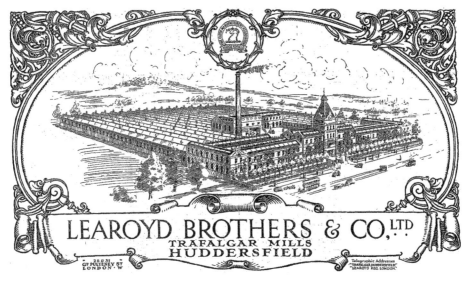

Trafalgar Mills from 1913 advertising.

archway to single-storey weaving sheds around a central quadrangle to enable clockwise progress of yarn to finished pieces. Designed by John Kirk & Sons, it got consent in January 1895 and opened as Trafalgar Mills in 1896 producing fancy worsteds.

The mill employed around 1,000 people. Despite repeated advice from a factory inspector only one of 190 looms had a safety guard. In 1898 a weaver, Florence Ellis, lost an eye when a shuttle flew from a loom. The company was summonsed under the Workmen's Compensation Act 1897 – a first under the act – and was fined 10s (50p).

A. E. Learoyd enjoyed a lavish lifestyle. In 1906 he had the innovative engineer Charles Binks open the Roydale (anagram) Engineering car manufacturing business at the mill. It made around twelve luxury cars with bodies built locally by Rippon Bros.

Learoyd's, by then part of Illingworth Morris, closed the 137,000 square feet mill in 1979. It is now home to Bevilacqua-owned CWF Continental Food and Wine Ltd.

Unlisted
See also Bevilacqua 7; Kirk 12;

37. Drill Hall, St Paul's Street

The Huddersfield volunteer corps was established in 1860. In need of a drill hall, it acquired the Theatre Royal, formerly a riding school (now the Colosseum, *see* 15) in 1863 where it was based until the opening of this purpose-built hall.

Architect Willie Cooper enlisted as a private in the volunteer corps in 1881 and had been promoted to captain by 1899. No surprise then that Cooper designed the building as headquarters of the 2nd Volunteer Battalion, the Duke of Wellington's Regiment. It was built on leased Ramsden land, paid for by public subscription of over £8,000 and is still held in trust for the local community.

The foundation stone was laid by Field Marshal Lord Roberts VC on 4 May 1899 and opened by General Sir Major Redvers Buller VC on 7 May 1901.

Drill Hall from Page Street.

Drill Hall interior with restored war memorials on the balcony and wall.

Built in a Tudor/medieval castle style in sneck-laid local stone, it has lots of historicist touches. The front's central bay has a tourelle on one side, a crenellated parapet to the other and a carved stone plaque of the regimental badge to the centre. The main entrance has timber gates set in arched gateway with mock drawbridge chain slots above. The upper segments of the gates form a mock portcullis. Other bays are embellished with tourelles and false cruciform arrow loops.

Behind is the 130 feet by 80 feet galleried hall with a timber-boarded roof, supported by wide-span, semi-circular trusses of laminated and bolted timber that rise up from the sprung timber floor.

The hall has been a venue for many public events including boxing, badminton and wrestling matches, dinners, dances, concerts, co-operative and union meetings, poor people's New Year treats, exhibitions and a women's suffrage ambush of the Secretary of State for War in 1907.

The hall has elaborate battalion war memorials with the names of the fallen, memorials that have been rescued from other sites and a 13 feet by 8 feet oil painting of the 1st/5th Battalion, Duke of Wellington's West Riding Regiment, a trench scene of holding the line at Ypres in 1915 by J. Hodgson Lobley.

The hall is an Army Reserve centre and HQ of the Corunna Company, 4th Battalion, the Yorkshire Regiment.

Listed grade II
See also Cooper 15, 32 & 35

38. Tramway Waiting Room, Edgerton Road

Huddersfield Corporation became the first municipal authority to operate a tramway service in 1883. In 1880 it had managed to keep control of its tramway through a Parliamentary Act but failed to find a company to lease the 10 miles of track it had laid by the end of 1882. From 1883, steam traction powered the Corporation's own tram cars. The Edgerton line started service in January 1884. In 1886 the Edgerton service was linked via Holly Bank Road to the Lindley line, forming a circular route. The service was electrified in 1901 and ran until 1939.

In September 1892 the Corporation introduced its first shelters – known as tramway waiting rooms – by commissioning six portable waiting rooms. The Corporation's General Purposes Committee established a Waiting Room Subcommittee that sought to arrange sites and the ordering of shelters. The first octagonal one was installed at Paddock in 1894.

There were soon requests for one at Edgerton but many of the lessees of the private park at Kaffir Road objected to one being sited there. It was not until July 1902 that the Corporation secured this site at Clayton Fields.

The classically detailed, pyramidal roofed and octagonal waiting room is the last of the network's shelters. It had lost its door by 1977 when it was Grade II listed.

In early 2014 the red-painted and dilapidated shelter was removed and restored by its owners, West Yorkshire Combined Authority, with consultants Aedas and joiners Stephen Metcalf Ltd of Accrington. On its return it was painted in the

Tramcar No. 29 of 1901/2 at Edgerton tram stop en route to Almondbury, after 1906.

Edgerton tram shelter, 2017.

Huddersfield Corporation Transport colours of vermillion and cream. It looked in fine form when the Tour de France passed by on 6 July 2014. It still serves as a bus shelter.

Listed grade II
See also AHR 1, 7, 30, 44, 46 & 50

39. Lindley Clock Tower, Lidget Street

What in 1899 made a seventy-five-year-old industrialist decide to replace four cottages with a £4,000, 83-foot clock tower on a street corner?

The inscription on the tower reads 'This tower was erected by James Nield Sykes Esq. J.P. of Field Head, Lindley, for the benefit of the inhabitants of his village in 1902.'

Whatever the reason his nephew, Edgar Wood, a Manchester architect, produced an Art Nouveau masterpiece. The straight standing stone tower is square in plan with slim diagonal buttresses that shoot through the steep pyramidal copper roof, all of which is an original design that delights local people.

The detailing also delights. Above the entrance a figure of Time stands on a winged world, holding a scythe and an hour glass, moving straight ahead. To his right is a figure of Youth, sowing seed; to his left is Old Age reaping. Above the figure of material Time is a winged figure standing on clouds and recording the acts of Time, while enshrined in the niche of Eternity.

Above: Details above the entrance of Lindley Clock Tower.

Below left: Lindley Clock Tower campanile.

Below right: Lindley Clock Tower from Plover Road.

On the buttresses by the 6 feet 6 inch clock faces are female figures of the four eternal virtues. Facing east is Truth with the book of truth and reflected in her mirror is Christ crucified. Her foot is Falsehood symbolised by a serpent. Facing south is Love, bearing her child in her arms over the thorny paths of life. Facing west is Purity with purifying torch and dove, standing on the flowing river, crowned with sweet-smelling bay leaf. Facing north is Justice, holding her scales perfectly balanced, and her sword, with her feet on Oppression and Vice.

There is also a relief frieze of the four seasons: to the east, spring with blossoming almond; to the south summer with rose; to the west, autumn with an apple; and to the north, winter with holly.

The gargoyles cantilevering from the four corners of the roof are The Beasts Fleeing the Tower of Time: the lazy, the vicious, the cunning and the greedy dogs. The copper and stone sculptural work was by a sculptor favoured by Wood, T. Stirling Lee.

The clock was started on Christmas Eve 1902. Sykes died on 4 March 1903. Perhaps the tower was his own memorial.

Listed grade II*

40. Post Office, Northumberland Street

Charles P. Wilkinson, an experienced Office of Works post office architect, designed the £30,000 three-storey building. Built of Elland Edge and Crosland

1914 Post Office from Lord Street.

Moor stone, it has a strong imperial presence on the street. A sweet Doric portico relieves the otherwise oppressive frontage.

Because of wartime emergency conditions it was opened without formality on 31 October 1914. Across the road from the smaller 1875 building, the whole block was given over to modern post office functions including telegrams, pensions, National Insurance and the administration of call boxes across the town. The telephone exchange on the top floor had roof lighting and its own staff staircase and facilities.

The public office was a classically inspired banking hall with marble dados and architraves, teak counters and bronze grilles, all now replaced with cheap materials. Only the coffered ceiling survives. There is a staff war memorial in the entrance.

The exchange was replaced by the Southgate automatic exchange in 1964. The three-storey modernist rear extension of 1968, a mechanised sorting office, used local ashlar and riven stone in harmony with its host. It is now a Royal Mail delivery office. Closure of the whole building is anticipated.

Listed grade II

41. Grand Picture House, Manchester Road

In 1883 an agreement between Huddersfield Corporation and the Hallidie Cable Company enabled the company to lease and run the town's first mechanical tram. It was to be a novel cable-driven system. Excavation started for the power house's

Grand Picture House façade.

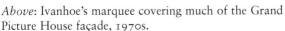
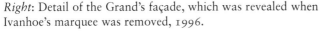

Above: Ivanhoe's marquee covering much of the Grand Picture House façade, 1970s.

Right: Detail of the Grand's façade, which was revealed when Ivanhoe's marquee was removed, 1996.

basement on Manchester Road. When the Board of Trade refused operating licences the scheme was abandoned that autumn, leaving just a large hole.

In 1919 work started in the hole on the Grand Picture Theatre, café and billiards hall. Designed by the architect Clifford Hickson of Stocks, Sykes and Hickson as a single-screen cinema, it has a façade of faience in a French Renaissance/Greek Revival style with Ionic columns. It opened in March 1921 with a capacity of 878.

Hickson also designed the 1915 Empire Cinema on John William Street and in 1922 a Northumberland Street warehouse conversion to the Princess Cinema.

The arrival of commercial television and trolleybuses from suburbs being rerouted up Outcote Bank led to a loss of trade and the Grand closed in June 1957. It became a bingo hall, then a dance hall as the Sheridan Rooms in 1960. In 1972 the balcony became the Hofbrauhaus and the hall Ivanhoe's nightclub with the cellar a disco, variously called Scamps, Antoinette, Flappers and Stripes.

Ivanhoe's was the venue of the legendary Sex Pistol's 1977 Christmas Day afternoon party for striking firefighters' and single parents' children, and an evening concert. It was the punk band's last UK gig before breaking up in Texas in January 1978.

In 1979 the building was bought by local insurance broker Dr Mohammed Eijaz Khilji, who reopened the cellar as the futurist Eros Nite Scene in 1980. It had 'computer-controlled' sound and lights and a stainless steel dance floor. There were ambitious plans for the hall as the 'main starship' but they crashed as Khilji was imprisoned for fraud. The building stood dark as the council assembled a retail development site. It was demolished in 1996, leaving just the elaborate façade that was revealed when Ivanhoe's marquee was removed.

Listed grade II
See also Hickson 21

42. Westgate House, Westgate

In 1902 architect Pascal J. Stienlet married Mary Stewart in North Shields. He became a prolific cinema architect in Newcastle with several partners including J. C. Maxwell.

In 1905 Norman Robinson, a Brockholes yarn spinning company director married Amelia Clough, daughter of a clothier of Haswell, Sunderland. In 1908 Robinson was a founding director of Huddersfield Town Football Club and until his death in 1943.

Amelia's brother Ernest served as lieutenant in France in 1916–17 where he was twice gassed, seriously injured and awarded the Military Cross. By the early 1920s Ernest lived with his sister and family on Smithy Place, Brockholes and later on Park Drive.

In 1923 Ernest commissioned Stienlet and Maxwell to redevelop the three-storey Paragon Hotel, on Chancery Lane, as a shop. The pub was demolished, leaving only one stone-built bay to the lane, and replaced with a steel-framed four-storey structure set back on a new building line. It is a remarkable classical, nouveau, deco and modernist confection. Set on a small plot, the ground-floor showroom has prismatic plate glass windows, and above are three-storey shallow

Below left: Westgate House.

Below right: Westgate House's recessed entrance with prismatic oak display cases.

iron oriels. Spaces between the windows are filled with moulded iron panels with cartouches and tiny Ionic columns. Above is an applied outsized san-serif 'WESTGATE HOUSE' under a deep classical cornice and flat roof. Inside the furniture and fixtures were of oak and glass.

The shop became 'Ernest Clough, high class gentleman's hatter and shirtmaker'. In 1933 Ernest moved into the top floor of Westgate House. He retired to Sidcup in 1973 and died aged eighty-five in 1977.

From 1976 to 2000 the Wade family owned the building and ran the business until closure in 1981 when the oak furniture was sold. International Fashions then sold women's wear until 1988. Subsequently an estate agent took up occupation and damaged the oak fixtures. Planning action followed, and the agent quit having made some repair.

It reverted to being an outfitters, Bronx, in 1993. Does the Stienlets' great-nephew, Sir Patrick Stewart OBE, actor, Huddersfield Town supporter and former chancellor of the University of Huddersfield, shop there and is his work shown in his great-uncle's cinemas?

Listed grade II

43. Police Box, No. 55 Northgate, Almondbury

This small blue box is the sole survivor of thirty-six Huddersfield miniature police stations that were brought into service in November 1930.

In 1929 the Huddersfield Chief Constable, Captain J. W. Moore, was faced with cuts in police force numbers and increasing demands on the force through

Borough architect Luther Smith's design for Huddersfield police boxes. (*Huddersfield Examiner*, 21 December 1929)

Above left: Almondbury police box with rooftop light, 1996.

Above right: Almondbury police box.

increased traffic duties and rising crime. In response he introduced 'automatic traffic signals' and decentralised officers with the boxes.

Every box had a telephone that was connected to the force's central Peel Street station that the public could use by opening a cupboard door on the box front. In another public cupboard were instructions on both phoning for an ambulance from the other cupboard and on first aid, with packets of gauze pads, bandages and iodine. A sign threatened improper use of the box could lead to a £20 penalty. On the arched roof was an orange lamp that could be lit remotely by the central police station to show a constable that his attention was required. If one was not in sight the public were encouraged to let a constable know the light was on.

All the boxes were painted Post Office red in accordance with Home Office instructions. They were painted blue later.

Inside each box was a desk, a stool, shelves, a stationery cupboard and a small electric stove. The boxes were used to detain arrested people until transport to a station could be arranged.

The Huddersfield boxes were designed by the borough architect Luther Smith in 1929 and built in wood by Wrigley & Beaumont, joiners of Linthwaite. The box was embellished with the borough's arms made by the Corporation's tramway department.

I don't have any reports of Huddersfield actress Jodie Whittaker being seen entering or leaving the box and *Doctor Who* enthusiasts may be disappointed because it only slightly resembles the television programme's TARDIS, which is based on the 1929 Gilbert MacKenzie Trench design.

The box was in occasional use until 2014. It was restored by West Yorkshire Police Estates Department in 2017.

Listed grade II

44. Renaissance Works, New Street

The town's co-operative society was founded as the Huddersfield Industrial Co-operative Flour and Provision Society in 1860. From the beginning it had a shop on this site.

The first surviving major development opened on Princess Street in 1887, designed by Abbey and Hanson. It set the free classical ornamental style for the New Street 1893 and 1906 extensions with a clock tower by Joseph Berry for which date stones can be found above wheatsheaves and other co-operative symbols, and the mottoes 'Labour and wait' and 'Unity is Strength'. The society bought the Victoria Temperance Hall in 1897. Now subsumed into the store, its roof can be made out at the back of Wilko. In 1906 the 1846 St Paul's School building was added to the estate.

Former Co-operative Society's central premises of 1887, 1893 and 1906.

Above: The 1937 Co-operative extension in 1956.

Below: The 1937 Co-operative extension in dereliction, from Chapel Hill.

The 1929 stock market crash led to difficult years. In the early 1930s the society planned a £125,000 extension, exhibiting a confidence in the movement. W. A. Johnson, the Co-operative Wholesale Society's chief architect, with assistant J. W. Cropper designed the extension that was the town's first truly modern building. It had a handsome composition. Steel-framed, clad with Crosland Moor ashlar between long horizontal ribbon windows and glazed stair bays, it must have been revolutionary for the May 1937 opening.

The co-op was then at a high point. It contracted over many years. In 1956 the extension failed to sell at auction for £60,000, and in 1963 Oastler College rented its upper floors and an unfortunate street canopy was fitted. Massive redevelopment was proposed in 1988. In 1999 the store closed and the building sold, with Wilko taking the pre-First World War part. The 1937 extension's lower floors were Heaven and Hell nightclub in 2002–04. Demolition in favour of new student housing threatened, but it was bought by Kirklees Council in a fit of redevelopment hubris for £2.1 million in 2007, a dreadful time to buy a derelict building. It took eleven years to get it off its hands. In 2018 SKA Developments started work on Renaissance Works, converting it into a 140-bed student housing with three additional storeys and extensions, using a multi-million pound loan from the Council.

Unlisted
See also AHR 1, 7, 30, 38, 46 & 50; SKA 24

45. Library and Art Gallery, Princess Alexandra Walk

Huddersfield was very late in opening a public library. There had been years of campaigning, debates and public polls but the Corporation was slow to act, prompting the 1891 tract *In Darkest Huddersfield and One Way Out Of It, or Why We Have No Public Library*. Eventually, in 1898 a public library and art gallery opened on the upper floors of Somerset Buildings (*see* 32). Soon more space was needed, so in 1934, the Corporation bought and cleared a site on Ramsden Street. E. H. Ashburner, principal assistant to the designer of the 1934 Sheffield Library, was appointed the project architect.

The 1940 building has echoes of Sheffield's design but Ashburner's work is like no other: neo-Egyptian, fascist, Grecian cinema in style.

Ashburner wrote in his *Modern Public Libraries: Their Planning and Design*:

I always feel strongly that in a library, perhaps more than in most buildings, it is incumbent of the architect to do his utmost to beautify his building by making it a permanent record of the best of contemporary art, sculpture, and other arts or crafts which are available. If artists of sufficient note are available locally, then so much the better – a further source of civic pride.

Above: Relief panel of inspiration leading to work, care and play by Woodford.

Left: Girl symbolising art, listening to the whispering voices of inspiration by Woodford.

Below: Central Library and Art Gallery.

He was true to his word. The materials used included Austrian oak, redwood, Burmah teak, gaboon, walnut, mahogany, cork, terrazzo, Swedish green marble (probably the last use of it in a UK public building), San Steffano marble and bronze.

The large Crosland Moor stone figures flanking the entrance steps, by the sculptor James Woodford, are *Youth awaiting inspiration*: a boy symbolising literature and a girl, art. Both are listening to the whispering voices of inspiration suggested by three relief panels on their thrones. Woodford also sculpted the relief panels below the first-floor windows, which show naked young people and children following caring, cultural and technical activities.

Other features by Ashburner have been covered or removed and lost by Philistines intending to 'update'. Paintings commissioned from Huddersfield School of Art teacher Reg Napier and students, for the children's library, have been restored and hung in the Local Studies Library.

The gallery rewards climbing the fine staircase.

Listed grade II

46. Bath House, Queen Street South

Established by the eponymous engineer in 1864, the family firm Thomas Broadbent & Sons Ltd made hydraulic and winding gear, and machinery for the textile industry. It now manufactures large scale industrial centrifuges and laundry equipment.

The 1953 legislation made it obligatory for UK iron and steel foundry workers to be provided with facilities for showering, changing clothes, drying and lockers. Thomas Broadbent commissioned the architects Abbey & Hanson to design such facilities for the company's ironworks. The project architect was Andrew Buck.

Planning consent was granted in April 1954. The building opened July 1955 and was in use until 2013. It is probably a unique survivor of the type and is a modernist architectural wonder. Its design was Buck's homage to Frank Lloyd Wright.

The building's strong horizontal and vertical lines are emphasised by the use of local sandstone, finely cut to various widths and finishes in diminishing courses, with the windows set in ashlar. The flat roof, reached by an external cantilevered steel staircase, had a sundeck, shelter and tank room.

Inside are 'clean' and 'dirty' men's locker rooms with showers in between. There were huge trough wash basins with foot-operated controls, electric shaver points, foot baths, a toilet block, an enamelled drinking fountain and all floors were terrazzo tiled. The basement's gas-fired boiler gave forced hot air and hot water heating systems, allowing drying in the vented lockers.

The builders were Law Stead & Sons, of which a director was Peter Stead, who showed great interest in Buck's design drawings. He was also building the local modernist masterpiece Farnley Hey and went on to design and build experimental houses, opened a gallery and became chairman of Huddersfield Civic Society.

Above: Broadbent's foundry amenity block, 2016.

Left: Off comes the dirt and grime as Mr J. S. Wells washes himself before going home. Amenity block, 1955. Note the driers, foot baths and foot-controlled taps.

Former amenities block interior, 2015.

The redundant foundry with amenity block or 'bathhouse' was bought by the University of Huddersfield, which demolished the foundry to erect the soon to be completed Barbara Hepworth building. In 2018 AHR plans were approved to renovate and convert the amenity block to the Bath House café and gallery. Opening is expected in 2020.

Listed grade II
See also AHR 1, 7, 30, 38, 44 & 50

47. Queensgate Market

In the late 1950s Huddersfield Corporation sought renewal of the town centre through Comprehensive Development Area powers. Murrayfield, its chosen developer, proposed new retail and offices, pedestrianised shopping with underground servicing, trees, raised flower beds, public art and a new market hall to replace the 1880 hall that lacked service areas with compromised access and food safety.

The Corporation retained its market charter rights but engaged Murrayfield's architect, the J. Seymour Harris Partnership, to design a market hall. The result was a hall generally hidden by being integrated with the Murrayfield development; however, it is unique with international provenance.

The project architect Gwyn Roberts and consulting engineer Joe Nicholls of Leonard and Partners took the work of the pioneering Spanish-born, Mexico-based architect Felix Candela and inspirational Austrian-born, Israel-based, MIT-trained engineer Elijah Traum to realise novel structures to roof and illuminate the market's 188 stalls.

The 1970 market's remarkable roof is formed of twenty-one hyperbolic paraboloid concrete shells constructed by Sir Robert McAlpine. Each shell is 56 feet by 31 feet, 10 feet deep and springs from a column 5 feet off-centre. Each of the structures is independent, without any bracing from neighbours. The 4 feet 6 inch vertical intervals between shells have clerestorey glazing that allows for independent movement of the shells. The sculptural shell soffits are reminiscent of the board-roofed stalls of outdoor markets.

Five of the shells towering over the ring road shelter a roof terrace to a never-opened mezzanine cafeteria.

Roberts trained at Birmingham Art School where he became friends with German-born, UK-based sculpture student Fritz Steller. Later Roberts gave Steller and his Square One Workshop of Stratford-upon-Avon an opportunity, for on the windowless wall on Queensgate are nine massive ceramic panels. These are *Articulation in Movement* that celebrates the shops inside, the goods of the market stalls and the asymmetric board-marked roof shells. Inside the market high on the north wall is another Steller work, the black-painted steel relief, *Commerce*.

A 2003 proposal of demolition by the Council led directly to it being listed in 2005 and it has since attracted the attention of architects artists, engineers, designers and ceramicists from around the world.

Listed grade II

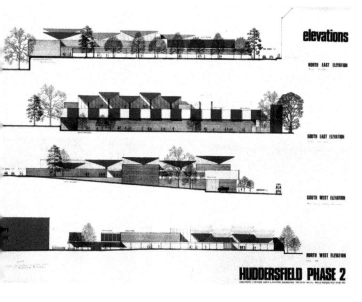

Architect's 1966 drawing of elevations of the proposed Huddersfield market hall.

Above: Queensgate Market from Queensgate, May 1970.

Below: Queensgate Market interior from the mezzanine, 2016.

48. HSBC Bank

It is said that Edward Hughes is Huddersfield's unluckiest architect, a comment on how many of his major buildings have been lost. One of them was his 1883 Huddersfield Banking Company (later Midland) building on the corner of Cloth Hall Street and New Street.

In 1970 it was replaced by another building, now HSBC, a five-storey geometric pattern of double beams and shiny planes that has been likened to both a tartan and a Chinese puzzle. The subtle rhythmic pattern of large bronze-tinted glass, polished granite oriels and bush hammered concrete distinguishes it as a building of great style from other commercial projects of its time in the town.

The two-storey banking hall has a drama from the apparent lack of structural support and glazed corner, which is achieved with minimal bronze window framing. There were concealed lighting tubes bringing a glow to the building in darkness. Inside the carpeted and air-conditioned banking hall was a chic blend of solid teak furniture and panelling, granite and rough concrete. Services were hidden in the twin beam structure.

The building structure and architectural statement was by Peter Womersley, working in partnership with Roger Shaw of Kitson & Partners to suit complex banking requirements.

Architect's concept of new Huddersfield Midland Bank, 1968.

Above left: HSBC branch from King Street.

Above right: One of six Atlantes and Caryatids in the HSBC banking hall.

In 1971 the granite was said to be 'Brazilian Old Gold', which is rather mysterious as it is not a material name that can be found in any other project. It was shipped from South America to Italy, and the blocks were sawn in Derbyshire and the panels cut and polished by Andrews in Leeds. There has been much change to the building in its short life. The painting of all the concrete has muted its appearance, the damage including turning the banking hall concrete a corporate HSBC red, which for some years gave it a rather alarming appearance. That has been replaced but the banking hall has been totally remodelled to meet modern practices. Delights that have survived from 1883 are six most exotic Caryatids and Atlantes from Exeter sculptor Harry Hems, which are remounted high above customers and are generally unnoticed.

Unlisted
See also Hughes 12, 13, 28, 30, 32 & 34

49. John Smith's Stadium

In the late 1980s the architects Lobb Partnership saw the need for new stadia design. Having developed their ideas with the engineers YRM Anthony Hunt Associates, Lobb presented the revolutionary concept A Stadium for the Nineties for the Sports Council at Birmingham's 1990 Interbuild.

Meanwhile in Huddersfield Graham Leslie, chairman of Huddersfield Town FC, and John Harman, leader of Kirklees Council, were developing a plan for a shared-ownership (association football and rugby league clubs with the council) and community-centred stadium to replace two unsafe and inadequate grounds.

Lobb won a limited Kirklees Council competition to design the 25,000-seat multi-use Kirklees Stadium complex. Derek Wilson and David Sheard of Lobb, and Stephen Murphy and Alan Bernau of YRM Anthony Hunt, led the realisation of a pioneering design, spectacular and colourful landmark that was to break the traditional design mould for stadia around the world – consider Stadium Australia, Wembley Stadium and others. The main contractor was Sir Alfred McAlpine. It was awarded the RIBA Building of the Year in 1995.

Work started in 1992 and the £15 million stadium opened in 1994. It is relatively intimate, oval in plan, with no seat more than 90 metres from the centre of play. The stands are roofed with the support of banana-shaped prismatic steel trusses spanning up to 143 metres and weighing up to 78 tons that spring from

John Smith's Stadium's Chadwick Lawrence Stand from the south.

A stadium concrete thrust block and legs and supporting a floodlight mast.

two pins on massive concrete thrust blocks, one at each corner. Each block is held aloft by four elegant smooth concrete legs and support floodlight masts, one with a finely detailed control box.

The four differing stands are architecturally cohesive and impressive. The apparently simple but actually sophisticated engineering has led to elegance. Set against the wooded landscape of Kilner Bank above, it seems to many not to be of Huddersfield.

The coming years are expected to bring a business class hotel, restaurants, bowling, dry slope skiing and other commercial uses to much more of the site.

The stadium has also been known through sponsorship as Alfred McAlpine (1994–2004) and Galpharm (2004–12).

Unlisted

5c. Oastler Building, Shore Head

The University of Huddersfield's latest project is neo-Googie and eye-catching, meeting the vice chancellor's demand: 'We want something architecturally striking – when students and parents come to the campus, I'm looking to give them the "wow" factor.' Architects AHR and main contractor Morgan Sindall delivered a project said to cost £28 million with a floor plan of over 7,000 square

Above: Oastler Building, University of Huddersfield, from Wakefield Road.

Left: Patterns of ashlar cladding to an Oastler Building lecture theatre above glazing, from Queensgate.

Central atrium from level four of the Oastler Building, University of Huddersfield.

metres. It provides well-equipped facilities for the Law School and much of the School of Music, Humanities and Media.

The building's name comes from Richard Oastler (1789–1861), the campaigner against child labour and slavery. Known as the 'Factory King' and 'King Dick', Huddersfield was his springboard.

It is on a most prominent site, forming a beacon for the university at a ring road junction. The curvaceous form has an atrium and galleried circulation that emulates the offices of major law and professional service companies. It includes four 300-seat lecture theatres.

It has some entertaining features. The five-storeys cantilever 3.5 metres, with each floor oversailing with LED 'neon' accents. This is said to self-shade the building's glass façade, reducing solar gain. Unfortunately the feature is most pronounced to the north-east and absent to the south.

Even more dramatic are the forty-two massive and elegant anodised aluminium brise-soleil fins – a so-called 'hockey stick' design that gives a toast rack look. Again the shading effect of these is questionable as they are arranged, giving glamour without purpose in some compass directions – architectural bling.

Approximately £200,000 of Crosland Moor stone as cladding is both interesting and dramatic. The stone is the vernacular building material but here it has been hung as ashlar smooth 30 mm slabs on vertical walls of the steel-framed building with 'neon' accents. It is also used in various thicknesses on soffits, fire doors and on a flat roof.

The building failed to win any architectural awards. There may be a moral here: form follows function.

Known affectionately as the 'Titanic', locals have been known to suggest that on a clear day, DiCaprio and Winslet can be seen embracing on the prow.

See also AHR 1, 7, 30, 38, 44 & 46

Further Reading

Balmforth, Owen, *History of Fifty Years' Progress 1860–1910* (Manchester, Huddersfield Industrial Society, 1910)

Brook, Roy, *The Story of Huddersfield* (London, McGibbon & Kee, 1968)

Browning, L., & Senior, R. K., *The Old Yards of Huddersfield* (Huddersfield Civic Society, 2004)

Chadwick, Stanley, *The Mighty Screen: The Rise of the Cinema in Huddersfield* (Huddersfield, Venturers Press, 1953)

Crump, W. B. & Ghorbal, Gertrude, *History of the Huddersfield Woollen Industry* (Huddersfield; Tolson Memorial Museum, 1955)

Gibson, Keith Booth, Albert, *The Buildings of Huddersfield; & An Illustrated Architectural History* (Stroud, Tempus, 2005)

Griffiths, David (Ed), *Making Up for Lost Time: The Pioneering Years of Huddersfield Corporation* (Huddersfield Local History Society, 2018)

Haigh, E. A. Hilary (Ed), *Huddersfield; A Most Handsome Town* (Huddersfield, Kirklees Cultural Services, 1992)

Haigh, E.A. Hilary, *Huddersfield Town Hall; An Ornament to the Town* (Huddersfield, Kirklees Council, 2001)

Harman, Ruth & Pevsner, Nikolaus, *The Buildings of England – Yorkshire West Riding: Sheffield and the South* (London, Yale UP, 2017)

Hobkirk, Charles, *Huddersfield: Its History and Natural History* (Huddersfield, Minerva Press, 1868)

Law, Edward J., *Joseph Kaye: Builder of Huddersfield* (Huddersfield Local History Society, 1989)

O'Connell, John, *The Making of a University: The Path to Higher Education in Huddersfield* (University of Huddersfield Press, 2016)

Redmonds, George, *Old Huddersfield 1500–1800* (Huddersfield, Redmonds, 1981)

Rennison, R. W., *Civil Engineering: Northern England'*, 2nd Ed (London, Thomas Telford, 1996)

Royle, Edward, *Queen Street Chapel and Mission, Huddersfield* (Huddersfield Local History Society, 2011)

Salveson, Paul, *Our Beautiful Station, Huddersfield 1847–2001* (Huddersfield, Penistone Line Partnership, 2001)

Stephenson, Clifford, *The Ramsdens and Their Estate in Huddersfield* (County Borough of Huddersfield, 1972)

Stocks, William, *Pennine Journey* (Huddersfield, Advertiser Press, 1958)

Walton, James, *Early Timbered Buildings of the Huddersfield District* (Huddersfield; Tolson Memorial Museum, 1955)

buildings.huddersfieldhistory.org.uk

discoverhuddersfield.com

homepage.eircom.net/~lawedd/index.htm

undergroundhistories.wordpress.com

Ackowledgements

Thanks to the owners and occupiers of the fifty buildings, the staff of Heritage Quay, the staff of Huddersfield Local Studies Library, the staff of West Yorkshire Archives (Kirklees), Anne C. Brook, Nathan Clay, Jamie Collier, David Griffiths, Brian Haigh, Martin Kilburn, Alan Rees, John Rumsby, Joseph Sharples, Roger Shaw, Mandy Sykes, Rudi Thramer, Sandra Wade and Simon Weldon.

Thousands of items have been consulted. Newspapers, archives, interviews and planning records have been key: *Bradford Observer, Huddersfield Chronicle, Huddersfield Examiner, Illustrated London News, Leeds Intelligencer, Leeds Mercury, Leeds Times, London Evening Standard, London Gazette, Yorkshire Post, Yorkshire Evening Post,* Huddersfield Local Studies Library enquiry folders, trade directories, Corporation and council minutes, and Huddersfield Corporation plans deposited.

All illustrations, unless otherwise attributed, are by Andrew Caveney in 2018, who reserves copyright. Either by the author or from his collection are pp. 15b, 16b, 22, 23b, 27t, 33t, 35b, 36b, 39t, 55r, 56t, 60b, 65b, 75, 78t and 86. The author and the publisher would like to thank the following people/organisations for permission to use copyright material in this book: Nathan Clay p. 10r; Dugdale Bros & Co. p. 50b; Stephen Haigh p. 83; Huddersfield Daily Examiner pp. 12t, 24b, 33b, 45r & 82b; Kirklees Theatre Trust p 20; James Lancaster/ CastlesFortsBattles.co.uk Copyright Reserved p. 9; Sir Robert McAlpine p. 85t; Propaganda p. 46r; Seymour Harris Architects p. 84; Sotnik & Dixon Collection pp. 27b, 31, 40t, 43b, 48r, 51r, 63, 68, 73 and 76l; Clifford Stephenson Collection pp. 14l, 17, 18r; George Webb p. 82t.

Every attempt has been made to seek permission for copyright material used in this book. However, if we have inadvertently used copyright material without permission/acknowledgement we apologise and we will make the necessary correction at the first opportunity.

About the Author and Photographer

Christopher Marsden was raised in Essex where he was weaned on Pevsner county guides. Educated at Bedales and Holme Valley Grammar, and Bristol and Leeds Polytechnics, he worked for thirty years in Kirklees Council libraries and communications. At the University of Huddersfield he enhanced his search and research skills with post-graduate marketing and an architectural history MRes on Queensgate Market.

In 2004 he co-founded Huddersfield Gem, which studied and campaigned on Huddersfield modernism. That led to him becoming a campaigning conservation secretary for the Tiles and Architectural Ceramics Society, chair of Huddersfield Civic Society and a Kirklees Historic Buildings Trust trustee.

Andrew Caveney is a professional photographer (www.creativedigitalphotography. co.uk). Having graduated with a BA (Hons) in Photography in 1988, he specialises in commercial and architectural photography. His work can be seen in many publications including *Pevsner Architectural Guides; Yorkshire West Riding: Sheffield and the South* (2017) and *The Villas of Edgerton* (2017). He lives in Birkby, Huddersfield. Away from photography, he is secretary of Huddersfield and District Beekeeping Association.